Their Lord and Ours

Their Lord and Ours

Approaches to Authority, Community
and the Unity of the Church

EDITED BY

Mark Santer

FOREWORD BY

The Archbishop of Canterbury

First published 1982
SPCK
Holy Trinity Church
Marylebone Road
London NW1 4DU

British Library Cataloguing in Publication Data

Their Lord and Ours.
　1. Church of England—Relations—Catholic Church
　2. Catholic Church—Relations—Church of England
　3. Christian union
　I. Santer, Mark
　270.8′28　　　BX9

　ISBN 0-281-04025-7

Photoset and printed in Great Britain by
Photobooks (Bristol) Limited
Barton Manor, St. Philips, Bristol

Contents

The Contributors

MARK SANTER is the Bishop of Kensington. He was formerly the Principal of Westcott House, Cambridge. He was a contributor to *The Phenomenon of Christian Belief* and the co-author of *Documents in Early Christian Thought*.

BARNABAS LINDARS SSF is the Rylands Professor of Biblical Criticism and Exegesis at the University of Manchester. His many published works include *New Testament Apologetic*, *Behind the Fourth Gospel*, *The Gospel of John* and *Church Without Walls* (ed.).

ANTHONY C. THISELTON is Senior Lecturer in Biblical Studies at the University of Sheffield. He is a member of the Doctrine Commission of the Church of England, to whose report *Believing in the Church* (1981) he was a contributor.

MARY TANNER is Tutor in Old Testament at Westcott House, Cambridge. She is an Anglican representative on the Faith and Order Commission of the World Council of Churches, and Theological Secretary of the Board for Mission and Unity of the General Synod of the Church of England.

KENNETH LEECH is the Race Relations Field Officer for the Board for Social Responsibility of the General Synod of the Church of England. His books include *Soul Friend*, *True Prayer* and *Youthquake*.

ROWAN WILLIAMS is Lecturer in Divinity at the University of Cambridge, and a Canon Theologian of Leicester Cathedral. He is also a member of the International Anglican Doctrinal Commission. He has written two books: *The Wound of Knowledge* and *Resurrection*.

JOHN MACQUARRIE is the Lady Margaret Professor of Divinity at the University of Oxford and Canon of Christ Church, Oxford. He is the author of many books, including *Christian Hope, The Humility of God, Christian Unity and Christian Diversity* and *Principles of Christian Theology*.

G. R. DUNSTAN retires in 1982 as the F. D. Maurice Professor of Moral and Social Theology in the University of London. His many published works include *The Sacred Ministry* (ed.), *The Artifice of Ethics* and *A Moralist in the City*.

Foreword

The Archbishop of Canterbury

In the theological ice-age each church had its cherished verbal formulas which it sought to impose on other churches. This attitude was understandable, since truth does not change, but recently we have become more acutely aware that our description of truth must always be subject to scrutiny. Words are the materials of the theological enterprise in which we seek to describe the truth, and words are alive and developing. They are unlike mathematical symbols in being inflected by their place in a living and changing culture.

The break up of the theological ice-age occurs when the historically conditioned character of our descriptions of the truth is fully recognized. Spring comes to the frozen wastes of ecclesiastical confrontation as we look, in company with fellow Christians, at the divine action and the events which give rise to our faith and seek to give their significance full value in terms of our contemporary language.

The Anglican–Roman Catholic International Commission has been attempting to follow this method and has made real progress. It is evident, however, that if the ice-field were to melt leaving only an inchoate ocean of private opinion very little would have been gained. Solid ground on which believers are able to take their stand is formed when the attempt to describe truth is made in the context of the believing community and with respect for previous formulations. In describing Christian truth we must beware both of frozen dogmatism and shapeless individualism. We establish firm ground, not by rejecting all the restraints of

ix

traditional expression, but by developing a theological method which is able both to stimulate and control individual exploration within the freedom and framework of the community of faith.

These essays, assembled at my suggestion under the editorial hand of Bishop Mark Santer, are a contribution to the search for such a theological method. They address themselves to their respective subjects in the same spirit which has guided the Anglican–Roman Catholic Commission in its work. They do not seek to rework the ARCIC agenda; rather they present us with some Anglican perspectives on related themes to the International Commission.

Bishop Mark Santer and the other contributors deserve the thanks of all those engaged in ecumenical dialogue, and I hope that *Their Lord and Ours* will stimulate wide study and discussion.

+ROBERT CANTUAR

1
Bible and Church

Barnabas Lindars SSF

One of the most encouraging signs in Roman Catholic and
Anglican dialogue today is the new approach to the Bible.
This can be described briefly as the recovery of the idea of
the Bible as the word of God. But this idea is freed from
untenable notions of scriptural inerrancy. Instead, it is
allied to full acceptance of the most rigorous criticism of the
Bible. Very often biblical criticism is regarded as totally
destructive of religious faith. Indeed it has too often been so
in the past, so that such fears are by no means groundless.
But recent tendencies give grounds for hope that it can be
used positively for revitalizing Christianity. Not only has
the Roman Catholic Church freed itself from crippling
restraints in the understanding of Scripture and doctrine,
but also the more conservative elements in the Church of
England, and indeed in the Protestant churches in general,
have begun to assimilate the results of criticism in a
constructive way which affords hope for the future. The
way is open for the degree to which the same problems cut
across the denominational barriers to be properly recognized, and for common work on the common task to begin.

It is not too much to say that there has been a revolution
in the understanding of the Bible in recent years. It is
completely different from the classic understanding of
Scripture, and this applies not only to the patristic and
medieval periods, but also to the Reformation. For, in spite
of all differences between them, throughout these periods
it was always presupposed that the Bible could and should
be interpreted in propositional terms. The contents of the

Bible, it was assumed, were equivalent to dogma. The classic position, held for centuries, took it for granted that the doctrine of the Church was in harmony with the teaching of the New Testament. Even the Old Testament was brought into line with it by means of typological exegesis. No formal distinction was made between Scripture and tradition. Before the Reformation, however, new tendencies of thought had introduced the idea that Scripture and tradition were comparable but separable, as if they were two sources of doctrine. This distinction was a vital factor in the controversies of the Reformation. It has also continued to hold Catholic and Protestant apart until very recent times. But it is now recognized on all hands to be untenable. The Bible is no longer assumed to be a handbook of doctrine, and the relation between it and the tradition of the Church is seen in terms of continuity and dynamic interaction.

The beginning of the two-source theory of Scripture and tradition has been ascribed to Henry of Ghent (died 1293), who suggested the theoretical possibility that the teaching of the Church might differ significantly from that of the Bible.[1] This apparently harmless suggestion opened the way to the theory that the tradition of the Church, which ideally is always in agreement with Scripture, is nevertheless not derived from Scripture, but directly from the apostles by oral transmission. This suited the canonists, who were bent on promoting the political power of the Pope, for it enabled them to evolve a doctrine of the papacy which would give the Pope a spiritual authority independent of criticism based on Scripture. They thus avoided the challenge of Wyclif, who was convinced that the manifest abuses of his time were proof that the Church had strayed from Scripture, and wished to place the authority of Scripture above the Church. Wyclif also shows the tendency to go for the literal sense of Scripture against the elaborations of allegorical exegesis in the prevailing spirituality. Thus attempts at reform and the recovery of the literal sense of Scripture tend to go together. On the other hand the maintenance of the status quo naturally relied upon tradition primarily, and tended to bring Scripture into line with it by continuing the long-standing methods of spiritual interpretation, derived from the Church Fathers. The revival of ancient learning in the fifteenth century led humanists such as Erasmus to reassert the classical position of the harmony of Scripture and tradition, but also to regard tradition as the guide to the interpretation of Scripture. Thus the power of the Pope over Scripture was not imperilled.

In all the complexity of thought of the later Middle Ages before the Reformation there is thus a polarization of Scripture and tradition which was clearly going to be a major factor in what happened then. Luther's rediscovery of the Pauline doctrine of justification by faith alone could not fail to set Scripture in opposition to the papacy as the embodiment of tradition. *Sola fide* leads to *sola scriptura*, as the whole of the Church's teaching and institutions are tested by the inexorable conflict between works and faith, law and grace. Thus the truly reformed position tended to claim the sufficiency of Scripture for salvation, and aimed at replacing ecclesiastical institutions with a new polity derived from Scripture without the intervention of tradition.

The continental Reformation was a matter of people rallying behind leaders, who inevitably formed new churches when their leaders were excommunicated. The Reformation in England followed a different pattern. Reform was in the air, and many churchmen such as Barlow and Latimer were deeply influenced by what was happening in Germany and Switzerland. But the schism with Rome came about neither by the influence of one great reformer nor by a decision of the hierarchy to follow Luther's lead. It was precipitated by the king. In desperation at failing to obtain papal dispensation to divorce Katharine of Aragon, Henry VIII took a leaf out of the reformers' book and denounced the Pope's jurisdiction in his realm. Otherwise he remained in intention

a Catholic. As Defender of the Faith he retained the prevailing Catholic view of the two sources of doctrine. Thus
the schism was not a victory for the Reformation point of
view, but the debate between Catholic and Protestant tendencies, already begun, now became an internal matter within
the schismatic Church of England. This resulted in a distinc-
tively Anglican position, but not without violent swings
and bloodshed. The Protestant party gained the upper hand
under Edward VI. The reversal under Mary I might have
succeeded, if she had not taken such drastic steps against
the Protestants and placed the country once more under
papal jurisdiction. This was a political misjudgement, if
nothing else. After the extremes of these two short reigns
the country needed above all things internal peace. This is
what Elizabeth I set out to give in the Act of Supremacy of
1559. Though the fires of controversy could not be quickly
quenched, and in the end the Calvinist wing could not be
contained within the Church of England, the reign of
Elizabeth saw a successful continuation of the debate which
had been begun under Henry. It is a debate which is
bounded by the *Apology of the Church of England* of John Jewel
in 1562 and the *Laws of Ecclesiastical Polity* of Richard Hooker
in 1594-7.[2]

In Hooker's work the Anglican position reaches its classic
expression. The theory of two sources of Christian truth,
Scripture and tradition, is retained. But these are seen to be
not really two independent sources of equal value. The
Bible is primary, and the authentic tradition is always in
harmony with it. This is indeed the view of the ancient
Church before the later medieval developments. But
Hooker places it within the setting of natural law, as a third
expression of the divine will. Against the Puritans, he
asserts that the Church cannot be reformed on the basis of
Scripture alone. Reason, Scripture and tradition (defined as
the decisions of the ecumenical councils of the undivided
Church, to exclude later errors) should be the guide to the
maintenance and renewal of the Church.

By opposing the single-source doctrine of revelation demanded by the Puritans, Hooker produced a view of the relation between Scripture and tradition which bears a certain similarity to the position which had already been reached by the Roman Catholic Church at the Council of Trent in 1546. As happens so often in such conciliar definitions, the decree was to some extent a compromise formula, hammered out after much passionate debate. In this decree it is stated that the gospel (as a matter of faith to be believed and discipline to be observed) 'is contained in the written books and in the unwritten traditions'. But the precise relationship between them remains ambiguous. It is implied that the whole gospel is contained in both sources. From this point of view the Bible is accepted as the primary source of doctrine, to be distinguished as a fixed literary deposit from the living tradition which interprets it. But the Bible is not the sole origin of the tradition, which stems from the word spoken through the apostles, even though they are in complete harmony.

Moreover the Council of Trent did not adopt the restrictive definition of tradition, common to Anglicans from Jewel to Hooker, which would confine it to the decisions of the undivided Church. And the practical need to defend existing church structures tended to draw the emphasis upon the *present* beliefs and practices of the Church as an expression of the gospel equally as valid as its expression in Scripture. Subsequent history reflects this difference of emphasis. In the Church of England the Bible became the book of the common people, supported, but not swamped, by the 'incomparable liturgy' of the Book of Common Prayer. In the Roman Catholic Church the Bible remained very largely the preserve of the clergy, and the institutions and teaching authority of the Church took the chief place.

Another factor, however, now enters the picture. The concentration of interest on the Bible, coinciding as it did with the recovery of ancient learning, was bound to lead eventually to the perils of biblical criticism. This showed itself first in the sphere of textual criticism. When the French Calvinist scholar Theodore Beza acquired the famous bilingual (Greek and Latin) manuscript of the Gospels and Acts (Codex Bezae Cantabrigiensis), he saw at once that it contained remarkable variants from the manuscripts previously known. Though he made some use of it in the second edition of his Greek text of the New Testament (1582), it was a long time before it was seriously considered. Meanwhile the text of the majority of manuscripts (the Textus Receptus) held sway, in spite of being an inferior text, and was duly accorded the exaggerated confidence which is inevitable with a doctrine of verbal inerrancy. Nevertheless the ground for a critical approach to the text of Scripture was being prepared by such monumental undertakings as Brian Walton's London Polyglot, in which the chief ancient versions were set out in parallel columns, following the example already set by the Complutensian Polyglot in Spain.

At the same time the dominance of the literal sense of Scripture in the reformed tradition inevitably drew attention to the discrepancies and other similar problems in the Bible. These could be avoided by harmonization to some extent, but were an obvious target for those who were critical of the spiritual value of the Bible as a result of developments in philosophy in the seventeenth century. It was the age of the dawning of scientific awareness. Rationalist thinkers, such as Lord Herbert of Cherbury, Thomas Hobbes and Spinoza, had sufficient detachment from the Bible to see its problems objectively, and were not slow to point them out. At the same time the new temper of mind encouraged a more scientific approach to the Bible even among those who were persuaded of its truth. Already in the late seventeenth century the Oratorian Richard Simon, a convert to Roman Catholicism, explained the growth of the Bible in terms of a literary history based on oral traditions. Naturally he fell foul of Bossuet, and his work was placed on the Index in 1682. But critical work on the Pentateuch was being done by another Roman Catholic, Alexander Geddes, a century later. By that time J. G. Eichhorn had produced the first critical introduction to the Old Testament (1780-3).

The important point here is the observation that the beginnings of the so-called higher criticism of the Bible were directly related to speculative currents of thought. In the early nineteenth century German romanticism pictured human history in terms of progress from primitive society to the peak of classical civilization. The Old Testament lent itself to interpretation along these lines. But this was bound to pose a threat to its value as divine revelation. Under the influence of Hegelian idealism W. Vatke presented the history of Israelite religion as the struggle of human consciousness to reach the Absolute. Interpretations of this kind naturally tended to reduce the spiritual value of the Old Testament. It might be supposed that the New Testament would escape a similar fate. But not a bit of it. The rationalist H. S. Reimarus, in a work published posthumously in 1778, had already proposed a naturalistic interpretation of Jesus as a messianic claimant who failed.[3] He supposed that the disciples stole the body of their crucified Master, and claimed that he had been raised up by God and thus divinely vindicated. This paved the way for the nineteenth-century notion of the New Testament as mythicized history. At Tübingen F. C. Baur used Hegel's ideas to explain the beginnings of the Church as a Jewish legalistic sect under Peter, which was opposed by the libertine Paul, and eventually resulted in the second century in the synthesis of the Catholic Church.

It can be objected that these works are not truly scientific. They are not based on careful sifting of the evidence, but on a preconceived theory of human history and religious development. But this would not be fair criticism, for they are pioneering attempts to relate the biblical data to the knowledge available at the time, and for this reason were bound to be highly speculative. But they aroused tremendous opposition from religious people. The reason for this was that they posed a threat to the supernatural character of the Christian revelation. Here were explanations of Christianity which tended to leave God out of account altogether. The problem is still with us today.

The reaction took the form of a reassertion of supernatural religion, either by exalting the privileged status of the Bible or by making higher claims for the Church as a divine institution. In the Roman Catholic Church it was possible to maintain that the practitioners of the higher criticism – all of them German Protestants – were the victims of their own inadequate version of Christianity. Here again was a view that has continued to the present time: that Protestantism leads to liberalism and private judgement, and eventually to the loss of supernatural religion altogether. It is not surprising that the beginnings of biblical criticism undertaken by Catholics such as Simon and Geddes now came to an abrupt end. The idea that the Church has charge over the interpretation of Scripture was strongly reasserted, and this had the effect of enhancing the supernatural character of tradition and magnifying the papal office. This tendency received powerful expression in the First Vatican Council of 1870, and became even more pronounced in the subsequent ultramontane propaganda.

The Church of England could not escape the threat so easily. Characteristically, those Anglican scholars who sought to make a reasoned defence against the new tendencies took up the patient and scientific work which had already been achieved in the 'lower' textual criticism, and extended it to the historical study of Christian origins. J. B. Lightfoot embarked on a massive study of the Apostolic Fathers, which was intended to correct the very late dating of the New Testament proposed by the Tübingen school by showing that the Catholic Church was fully formed by the end of the first century. It is a sign of the times that he published a collection of individual studies on the ancient Church under the title *Essays on Supernatural Religion*. These and similar studies had the effect of emphasizing the continuity between Scripture and tradition. The two sources are now seen to be one source – the New Testament with its subsequent theological development. It may be remarked in passing that the Catholic revival in the Church of England at this time is another assertion of supernatural religion, comparable to the exaltation of tradition in the Roman Catholic Church. But the doctrine of the Church associated with it was significantly different. Though many Anglo-Catholics were influenced by post-Tridentine spirituality, their concept of the Church could never carry with it the confidence with which the Roman Catholic Church claimed the *present* state of the Church as the true social embodiment of the gospel. To them the overriding consideration was continuity with the past, faithfulness to the message once delivered to the saints.

Meanwhile the Evangelical wing of the Church of England sided with other Protestants in upholding the literal inerrancy of Scripture against the biblical critics. From this time biblical fundamentalism, which had always been the general assumption before the rise of criticism, became a distinctive position, and indeed the hallmark of a converted Christian. But there was little creative dialogue, so that the hermeneutical problems were not faced. Biblical fundamentalism thus appears more a matter of decision than of reason. It is the necessary corollary of personal allegiance to Jesus as Lord and Saviour. The experience of salvation persuades the individual that Jesus is God. This fact is the guarantee of the divine origin and absolute trustworthiness of the Bible. It is easy to dismiss this stance as a 'retreat to commitment', but its immense power and persistence deserve recognition.

All of these responses to the threat to supernatural religion can now be seen to be over-reactions. As the century wore on, biblical criticism began to make its way in orthodox circles. The excesses of the Tübingen school were discredited. The accumulation of new knowledge gave promise that the Bible could be placed in its proper historical context, and definitive solutions to the problems raised by earlier critics appeared to be within the grasp of scholarship. The Germans still led the way, but in England, Scotland and America there were notable contributions to research. Even in the Roman Catholic Church efforts were made to assimilate the new knowledge constructively, especially in the work of Lagrange and his establishment of the École Biblique at Jerusalem. The papal encyclical *Providentissimus Deus* of 1893 reasserted the Church's claim to be the sole arbiter of scriptural interpretation, but was careful to leave the way open for the pursuit of scientific research.

The present century therefore started on a hopeful note. In England the results of biblical criticism were made available to the general public by men of acknowledged Christian conviction such as the Primitive Methodist A. S. Peake and the Anglican Charles Gore. But the turn of events in the Roman Catholic Church was little short of tragic. Alfred Loisy attempted to answer the reductionism of the liberal German critics by making a sharp separation between the non-supernatural interpretation of the Gospels revealed by historical scholarship and the divinely guaranteed doctrine of the Church. Scripture and tradition were thereby split apart into two irreconcilable entities. The suspicion that biblical criticism leads necessarily to the denial of supernatural religion was confirmed. Loisy was branded as a Modernist, and excommunicated in 1908. Thereafter Roman Catholic biblical scholarship was placed under rigid control. Scarcely any room was left for the integration of the results of critical study with the teaching of the faith. This effectively smothered the message of the Bible itself, because the interpretation of it was guided entirely by dogmatic presuppositions.

The 'Babylonian captivity' of biblical studies in the Roman church came to an end with the accession of Pope

Pius XII, whose encyclical *Divino Afflante Spiritu* (1943) removed all restrictions and encouraged co-operation between Catholic and Protestant scholars. Much of the credit for this bold reversal of policy is due to the patient work of Cardinal Agostino Bea, the former rector of the Pontifical Biblical Institute. Indeed it is probable that he wrote much of the encyclical himself. Born in 1881, he had grown up in the period of the hopes engendered by the encyclical of Pope Leo XIII in 1893. In an essay written in the centenary of his birth, it is fitting to pay special tribute to his achievement.

Catholic scholars exercised their new freedom cautiously to begin with, tending to side with the more conservative among the Protestant critics. Moreover, continuing anxiety about the perils of liberalism came to the surface once more in 1958, after the death of Pius, in what has been described by one Roman Catholic Scholar as 'an incredible and savage campaign . . . against all critical Biblical study'.[4] Consequently the full force of the encyclical was not felt until after the Second Vatican Council. The original schema *De Revelatione*, presented in 1962, still clung to traditional notions of scriptural inerrancy. Only after much debate and four further revisions was a final draft approved (*Dei Verbum*, 1965) which left the question of the nature of scriptural inspiration sufficiently open to accommodate the results of critical study. But this draft was accepted by such an overwhelming majority that there could be no further doubt that the complete freedom recommended by *Divino Afflante Spiritu* represented the mind of the Church on this issue.

The decision of the Council has been fully justified by events. In the first place, Catholic scholars have indeed co-operated fully with Protestants in biblical studies, to the great benefit of the common search for truth. Secondly, the renewal of all aspects of Christian life and spirituality associated with Vatican II has included a real discovery of the Bible by the people. This has been promoted at the very centre of church life by the enormously increased use of the Bible in the new liturgical forms. This includes the restoration of Old Testament lessons in the Mass, the provision of responsorial Psalms, and the systematic reading of the Bible in the Office of Readings and other parts of the Daily Office. Thirdly, this in its turn has produced a demand for popularization of the results of the past century of Bible study, and Catholic scholars have been ready and equipped to supply this need. The massive *Jerome Biblical Commentary* published in England and America in 1968, and now used and valued by students of all denominations, is entirely the work of Roman Catholic scholars, designed deliberately to show that Roman Catholic scholarship is in no way inferior to the work of contemporary Protestant scholars. Thus knowledge of the Bible is reaching the people to a degree that those outside the Roman Catholic Church may well envy. Naturally it has also brought to people's attention the central message of the gospel itself. This may well have profound consequences.

The task of bringing the results of biblical scholarship to the people at large is more difficult than appears at first sight. There is no such thing as 'assured results'. Popular demand for certainty has to be replaced by a proper understanding of the provisional nature of much critical work, and a deeper appreciation of the nature of religious assurance. Popularization requires sensitivity to the delicacy of the task and a strong sense of responsibility on the part of scholars. The new generation of Roman Catholic scholars deserves the greatest credit from this point of view. Sadly, the same cannot be said of all Anglican scholars who undertake work of this kind. Too often Anglican theologians descend to blockbusting and sarcastic ways of writing, which are no doubt intended to provoke and stimulate thought, but are more likely to produce disturbance and confusion in the minds of their readers than the excitement of acquiring new knowledge and fresh insights.

The rediscovery of the Bible associated with Vatican II

has also influenced some contemporary movements within the Roman Catholic Church. One of these is the liberation movement in Latin America. This draws its inspiration from the Exodus tradition in the Old Testament and its moral urgency from the teaching and example of Jesus himself. It is also true that the political analysis of the liberation theologians, derived from Marxism, has influenced their reading of the Bible. If this runs counter to traditional teaching, it can be claimed that this is only to be expected when the Bible is allowed to speak for itself. Thus the release of the Bible from strict control of interpretation carries with it the need for the most serious endeavour to establish the real meaning of the Bible and to show the limits of what may be properly deduced from it. Biblical scholarship is essential if the Bible is not to be abused.

Similarly the pentecostal movement in the Roman Catholic Church (now believed to number up to four million adherents)[5] is heavily dependent on the Bible. The movement can be described as a rediscovery of the joy and assurance and generosity of the creative, pioneering days of the Church, as depicted in the Acts of the Apostles and the letters of Paul. Here there is the danger of a naive fundamentalism with regard to the New Testament, which owes far more to the Protestant tradition than to the Catholic fundamentalism of the period before Vatican II. As before, the movement needs not only inspiration from the Bible but also the restraining influence of a sound understanding of the Bible. If the aim is to recapture the explosive force of the original experience of Christianity, it must make sure that it is the real thing, rather than the enthusiasm of romantic imagination.

These considerations lead to the question of biblical inspiration, which has been the subject of much debate within the Roman Catholic Church as a result of Vatican II. In what sense is the Bible the word of God? The idea of verbal inerrancy, long debated in the past, has been

13

successively modified and finally abandoned. Modern form criticism, concentrating on the different types of literature within the Bible, and the processes of their transmission, has shown that a literal interpretation is often a mistaken understanding of the writer's intentions anyway. So the concept of inspiration has been attached to the intention of the writer. As one inspired by the Spirit of God, he infallibly conveys the truth of God in what he actually has to say. But this view does not allow for the complexity of the Bible, where there may be an important distinction between the intention of an editor or redactor and that of his sources. In what sense is the prophecy of the Immanuel child in Isaiah 7.14 the word of God? Is it in the meaning originally intended by the prophet (probably a symbolic way of giving assurance of relief from political pressure)? or to the redactor (who makes it suggestive of destruction)? In any case, neither of these are the same as the christological meaning attached to it in the New Testament.

Another modern Roman Catholic view is the concept of the *sensus plenior*, promoted especially by P. Benoit. This retains the idea of verbal inspiration by applying it to the truth which God speaks through the instrumentality of the sacred writers. On this view the word of God in the Immanuel prophecy is not fully disclosed until it is reinterpreted in relation to the Christ event. The principle can be extended to cover the further development of doctrine on the basis of the biblical texts. But it is not altogether satisfactory, because the inspiration then belongs more to the exegesis than to the texts themselves. Moreover there is an inevitable tendency to devalue the Old Testament, which becomes merely preparatory to the divine message given in the New Testament. But surely, if there is a sense in which the Bible is the word of God, it applies in some way to the Old Testament as well.

One more way of retaining a modified concept of verbal inspiration has been put forward by N. Lohfink. This is a variant of the last view, in that the infallible truth of God can be discovered only when the Bible is taken as a whole. But instead of attaching the concept to specific texts, Lohfink sees it in the relation of all parts of the Bible to the whole. Taken individually, large tracts of Scripture have little to offer in the way of divine revelation, and indeed there is much material which expresses primitive and frankly brutal ideas about God himself. But these all contribute to the salvation history, whereby the truth of God, accommodated to the different capacities of men to apprehend it, was gradually revealed. The objection remains that the Old Testament is inevitably depreciated along this line of thought.

What is needed is a much more dynamic idea of the Bible as the word of God. Here we can see a very promising convergence of approaches, both Catholic and Protestant. The principle is that God is found to be speaking *both* within the Bible to the original hearers *and* through the Bible to the Church today. This view is found in an array of Protestant theologies, which includes most of the great names of modern theology. Barth and Brunner, Bultmann and Tillich, Pannenberg and Moltmann, all see the Bible in terms of personal encounter between God and man. In every case the encounter demands an existential response. This is how the word of God operates in the prophets of Israel. It is specially true of Jesus himself, and continues in the explosive impact of the Christ event. Furthermore, it overcomes the problem of the successive layers of the Bible from a literary point of view. For this dynamic understanding of Scripture applies both to the fundamental sources in their original setting and to the subsequent work of revision, whereby the old traditions were made relevant to later situations in Israel's history. Biblical criticism not only exposes each different layer, but also helps to remove the wrappings which so often blunt the message in the process of domesticating the original traditions. This has been an especially important factor in research into the life of Jesus. The modern picture of Jesus presents a flesh-and-blood

personality far more challenging than the sweetness of
Catholic oleographs or the ethereal presence of Protestant
art.

One obvious objection to this approach is that, if
existential encounter is the decisive factor in the long
history of Israel and on into the New Testament, it seems
arbitrary to stop there. Did God cease to speak at the end of
the apostolic age? This question takes us once more to the
problem of Scripture and tradition. But now the relationship between them can be put in another way. The New
Testament is the record of the happening in which the
Church came into being. In spite of all the complexities of
the formation of the canon, the fact remains that the New
Testament is the chief literary expression of the first
Christian century and the primary source for our knowledge of the beginnings of Christianity. It is, then, the only
thing approaching a reliable record of how God spoke to us
through his Son (Heb. 1.2). The Church is the body of those
who have been baptized into the name of Jesus, the
community of those who acknowledge him as their Lord
and Master. Hence the tradition of the Church may be
defined as the faith and practice by which the Church has
attempted to live under his lordship through the centuries.
When God speaks to the Church, by whatever means, his
word has an essential relationship with his Word in Christ
simply because of what the Church is. The Word of God in
Christ does not only belong to the past, but also to the
future. The Christ event has an eschatological dimension.
The future of man has been declared and achieved in
advance in the person of Christ. Thus, as the Church moves
forward through time towards the consummation of what
has been accomplished in him, the word of God to the
Church recalls it to its origin in Christ for the sake of its
future in Christ.

The tradition of the Church, its faith and practice, is a
history of obedience and disobedience, of blindness and
illumination, of glory and shame, comparable to the history

of the people of God in the Old Testament. The Spirit of God, who was active in the prophets, creating by means of threats and promises the conditions for the coming of Christ, is active in the Church now, creating the present day of Christ that leads to the consummation in Christ. It is even possible to speak of the time of the Church as the era of the Holy Spirit, though not in the sense claimed by Joachim of Fiore. For the Old Testament period was also in a true sense the era of the Spirit, and on the other hand the present activity of the same Spirit does not permit a triumphalist view of the Church, moving majestically towards the consummation, for his activity can still be just as much to denounce sin as in the prophets of old. It is the fact that God's purpose is already achieved in Christ which gives assurance that the Church cannot ultimately fail.

This dynamic view of the word of God in Scripture leads to a functional view of its purpose. The Bible exists to recall the Church to God through Christ. This is in fact what is happening in those circles of the Roman Catholic Church where the rediscovery of the Bible is strongest. And precisely because it must be the real Jesus, and not a distorted imaginative view of him, that is at the centre, biblical criticism is essential to provide the corrective and lead, as far as can be done, to the reality of God's message in Jesus and the emergence of the Church. It is also encouraging to note that the Evangelicals have gone a long way to accepting biblical criticism from this point of view.

The two-source theory of revelation, which was such a powerful factor at the time of the Reformation, is dead. Not only is it wrong to think of the tradition of the Church as a separate source, but the Bible itself is not to be thought of as a source of information but as God's way of addressing the Church today. But this does not mean that the Bible has nothing to do with doctrine. On the contrary, it means that doctrine is to be seen as the explication of the Christ event, and therefore must be continually tested by the Bible as the record of that event. The rediscovery of the Bible in the

Roman Catholic Church is bound to have its effect upon doctrine, not only upon formal dogmatic statements, but much more on the way they are felt and imagined by the people. A Roman Catholic writer has observed that the Roman Catholic Church has yet to face 'the sensitive problems of New Testament exegesis that have vital dogmatic implications, e.g. the limitations of Jesus' knowledge regarding himself, the future and the Church; the reliability of Acts as a guide to how the Church historically emerged . . . the historicity of the infancy narratives.'[6]

But it is not only in the Roman Catholic Church that such issues have to be faced. They are at the centre of debate in all the main churches. The current controversy concerning the incarnation has been pending since the rise of biblical criticism. But the solution will not necessarily take the form of abandonment of supernatural religion. As the processes whereby Christian doctrine developed in explanation of the Christ event become better understood, so the way is opened for fresh understanding of doctrine through sharing the experience which brought it to expression. The need today is not to jettison tradition and attempt to start again (that was a mistake made at the Reformation), but to work patiently back through tradition to the origins. This will show how far the doctrines match the experience, and the extent to which fresh formulations must be found in order to express it today. This is a matter of the utmost importance, for the experience of God's act in Christ is the gospel which has been entrusted to the Church for the world.

This task is the common task of Christendom today, and nothing is gained by attempting to perform it in watertight compartments. The encyclical *Divino Afflante Spiritu* specifically recommended co-operation between Catholics and Protestants in the study of the Bible. This should be extended to greater co-operation at every level. The word of God to the Church does not exist to buttress the present form of the Church. It exists to recall the

Church to its origin in Christ for the sake of its future in
Christ; to create now the present day of Christ that leads to
the consummation in Christ.

NOTES

1   G. H. Tavard, *Holy Writ and Holy Church* (Burns & Oates 1959),
    p. 23.

2   Books I–IV of Hooker's *Treatise on the Laws of Ecclesiastical Polity*
    were published in 1594 and Book V in 1597. Three further
    books appeared posthumously in 1648 and 1662.

3   Reimarus is the first author reviewed by Albert Schweitzer in
    his classic *Von Reimarus zu Wrede* (1906; English translation *The
    Quest of the Historical Jesus*, 1910).

4   B. Vawter, *Biblical Inspiration* (Philadelphia and London 1972),
    p. 126.

5   R. Laurentin, *Catholic Pentecostalism* (Darton, Longman and Todd
    1977), p. 15.

6   J. S. Kselman, article on 'Modern New Testament Criticism' in
    The Jerome Biblical Commentary (Geoffrey Chapman 1968), II,
    pp. 7–20.

2

Academic Freedom, Religious Tradition, and the Morality of Christian Scholarship

Anthony C. Thiselton

The phrase 'the morality of scholarship' denotes an area of ethical problems which are by no means peculiar to the academic study of Christian theology. In 1967 a philosopher of language published a collection of essays under this title which made little or no mention of problems of theology or of Christian faith.[1] The essays discussed the moral constraints experienced by sociologists, philosophers and political theorists, who were simultaneously committed to teach their subject with appropriate rigour and objectivity, and also committed as human beings or as citizens to certain practical, social or political programmes.

An examination of the growing body of literature on the morality of scholarship outside the distinctive context of Christian theology brings several fundamental principles to light. First, it is a mistake to construe the long and bitter debates about the academic study of theology simply as a struggle to wrest academic freedom from the clutches of a defensive religious dogmatism. The debate is not simply a matter of personal integrity *versus* church doctrine. Moral issues and moral constraints emerge on *both* sides of the debate. The Christian scholar belongs to more than one community, and membership of each community carries with it certain moral obligations towards the community in question. Second, we can no longer take for granted what is meant by 'objective' academic scholarship. Admittedly appeals to re-define this concept have sometimes been little more than a shallow propagandist device to give subjectivism or dogmatic prejudice some pretended veneer of academic respectability. It may offer a supposedly rational argument for an irrational position. But at a deeper level, the debate in the social sciences and in hermeneutical theory about the limitations of value-free knowledge constitutes a proper and urgently necessary dimension of the discussion. Third, an over-simplistic view of the debate about academic freedom and the morality of scholarship has sometimes seemed plausible on the basis of an unduly individualistic understanding of the nature of scholarly enquiry. The simplistic model of the scholar is that of the lone individual pioneer cutting through the errors of tradition and arriving on his own at some startling novelty. But creative scholarship in actual practice takes place *within* the framework of a tradition and of the knowledge of the community, and scholarly creativity involves something far more profound than mere novelty.

This chapter is an attempt to bring these three factors to bear on the otherwise well-worn debate about academic freedom in theology, in the hope that we may then be in a better position to see what *both* sides in the debate are trying to say. The really interesting and urgent debates in theology are not usually those in which all of the best arguments seem to be on the same side. It is when we wish somehow to say 'Yes' to *both* sides of an argument which seems, at least in popular thought, to offer incompatible alternatives, that we are encouraged to continue to wrestle with a familiar problem. This is certainly the case with the present subject. If theology is removed from the realm of genuinely objective, rigorous and critical academic study, Christians lose their claim to intellectual integrity and

21

honesty. Theology would then have retreated into a ghetto world of mere propaganda. On the other hand, the Christian scholar remains a Christian and a human being whose faith is nourished, and whose actions are directed, by the tradition to which he belongs and the God whom he worships. An 'ivory tower' scholar is one who forgets that as a human being he experiences constraints and recognizes concerns which make claims upon him above and beyond those of the academic community. No one would condone, for example, a scholar's spending so long at his desk as to become an irresponsible and unloving parent on the ground that his commitment to the pursuit of truth was all that mattered to him as a scholar.

The variety of standpoints represented in the debate

Do all Christian scholars experience the problems and tensions which are implied by the history of the present subject? Certainly some find no tension at all between the demands of Christian discipleship and the expectations of the academic community. One well-known and eminent British biblical scholar makes this point explicitly and strikingly in a recently published autobiography. F. F. Bruce writes: 'I am sometimes asked if I am aware of the tension between my academic study of the Bible and my approach to the Bible in personal or church life. I am bound to say that I am aware of no such tension . . . There is no conflict between my critical or exegetical activity in a university context and my Bible exposition in church . . . The Christian acceptance of the Bible as God's word written does not in the least inhibit the unfettered study of its contents and setting.'[2] Bruce underlined the importance of academic freedom in 'this subject of all subjects' in his inaugural lecture as professor of Biblical History and Literature in the University of Sheffield, noting that in the context of the university his commitment in teaching Biblical Studies was the same as what it had been when in earlier years he had lectured in classics: 'one's only commitment is to truth . . . to follow the evidence wherever it leads, in an atmosphere of free enquiry.'[3] Even though his own theology is conservative rather than radical, he expresses a strong preference for the environment of the university as over against that of the theological seminary.

By contrast, however, another British theologian, Donald MacKinnon, offers a diametrically opposite verdict concerning the presence or absence of tension between academic freedom and Christian commitment. Like F. F. Bruce, he insists that 'it is of course essential for the health of theology as a subject that it should be carried on in the setting of a university, and not be in the restricted, specially orientated atmosphere of a denominational seminary.'[4] But part of the reason for this is that the cross-fertilization with ideas flowing from other fields of study should serve to stimulate a sense of *restlessness* and *discontent* with theology as a task completed and adequately done. It stands in the Reformation tradition of *ecclesia reformata semper reformanda*. The sense of pressure and tension which are made by the simultaneous demands of Christian faith and academic openness make the academic theologian 'a rootless man, restless and awkward, ill at ease with himself . . . It should not be easy to be a theologian in a modern university; indeed it should never have been easy . . . Theology lives through interrogation.'[5] MacKinnon concludes by comparing the pain and tension which is inescapable for the academic theologian with the inescapable signs of costly and authentic apostleship experienced by Paul in the struggles reflected in 2 Corinthians.

The history of the debate witnesses to a degree of controversy and passion which underlines the genuineness of the problems posed by our subject. Since at least the time of Clement and Origen, on the one hand, and of Tertullian, on the other, Christians have debated the extent to which theology should be done within the distinctive context of the Church alone or also within the wider context of man's universal quest for truth wherever it is to be found. G. R. Evans and others have traced the history of the debate about the status of theology as an academic discipline to the era of the foundation of the universities in twelfth-century Europe. Evans cites the notorious public conflicts between the 'academic' approach of Peter Abelard and Gilbert of Poitiers and the Church's 'defender of the faith' in the person of Bernard of Clairvaux.[6] Wolfhart Pannenberg also dates the beginnings of theology as an academic discipline from the twelfth and thirteenth centuries, arguing that its scientific status as a university subject is part and parcel of a wholly proper and necessary concern that the truth of Christianity should be seen publicly to stand the test of 'generally accepted criteria'.[7]

A number of writers including from a Lutheran perspective Gerhard Ebeling and J. Pelikan, and from a more Calvinist or Barthian standpoint T. F. Torrance, have rightly urged that the academic context of theology as a scientific discipline was of fundamental importance to the Reformers. We shall look more closely at this argument in due course. When we move, however, into the post-Enlightenment era, and especially into the controversies of the nineteenth century, it is clear that the debate has become transposed into a new key which sadly allows and even invites polarization into two bitterly opposed camps. As a sample of the issues which came to the surface most characteristically in this nineteenth-century era, we may briefly allude to four well-known episodes.

First, the foundation of the University of Berlin in 1810 was preceded by a sharp debate in 1807 between Friedrich Schleiermacher and the philosopher J. G. Fichte about the status of theology in the university. Standing in the tradition of philosophical idealism, Fichte saw theology as the handling of ideas which should be taught in the university as a purely academic subject, without reference to any ecclesiastical or dogmatic context. Schleiermacher, on the other hand, stood in the tradition of Romanticism with its emphasis on 'life' and 'experience'. He refused to reduce religion, as a phenomenon of human life, to 'theology', as the abstract, objectivist study of ideas or concepts. Hence he urged that theology or religious studies should take its place within the university as a vocational or applied subject, oriented towards ministerial training. To train competent clergy, he argued, lay no more outside the province of a state university than any other course of study which equipped the professional leaders of the nation to perform their role in the national community. He believed that this principle in no way compromised the necessary distinctiveness of the Church over against the state or society in general.

If Berlin brought into focus one aspect of the nineteenth-century debate, the University of Halle served as a focus for another. In 1810 Wilhelm Gesenius became Professor at Halle. But the devout and orthodox of the German church saw his teaching and writing as an intolerable example of the excesses and destructive effects of the application of Enlightenment rationalism to biblical studies. In 1830, which was the Jubilee year of the Augsburg Confession, E. W. Hengstenberg published a bitter attack on Gesenius on behalf of church orthodoxy. A long and biting public debate took place, in which one major theological issue became that of whether the questioning of church tradition was entailed as a fundamental of the theology of the Reformation. So widespread was public concern over the debate that a report was submitted to the Prussian King, even though in the event no actual legal proceeding was taken against Gesenius.

A third facet of the nineteenth-century debate appears in the careful enquiries which took place among scholars more moderate than Gesenius but less cautious than Hengstenberg, about the scientific status of biblical studies. Wellhausen's teacher, Heinrich Ewald, provides a notable example of a scholar who at one and the same time rejected the radical extremes of F. C. Baur and D. F. Strauss, but also insisted on the necessity of using scientific method in biblical studies.

Finally, in England and the English-speaking world these issues came most strikingly before the public eye with the publication in 1860 of the volume entitled *Essays and Reviews* and through the work of Bishop J. W. Colenso of Natal. Bishop Colenso was censured by the English bishops, and many leading figures were drawn into a widespread and often harsh debate about subscription and assent to the Articles of Religion of the Church of England. Up to this period, assent to the Articles was required from members of the older universities proceeding to degrees. In the ensuing debate Benjamin Jowett, one of the contributors to *Essays and Reviews*, argued for the abolition of the university tests on the ground that those who were genuinely free to speak what they believed without constraint from the Church could do so with greater authority and effectiveness than if matters were otherwise.

Although university tests as such were indeed abolished, the Church of England has always retained the requirement for assent to its doctrine on the part of its clergy. The lay theological scholar stands in a different position from the scholar who is also the holder of a teaching office within the Church of England. Arguments for and against subscription on the part of the clergy feature in Reports of the Church of England Doctrine Commission in 1938 and most recently in 1981.[8] Indeed the 1981 Report reaffirms the traditional Anglican standpoint that while the integrity of the individual theological explorers must be respected, there are definite limits to the freedom that can be enjoyed by those who are authorized to teach and to minister 'in the Church's name'.[9]

Today the debate is as wide-ranging as ever, and embraces still the widest possible divergence of views. Perhaps the most startling contrast can be achieved by comparing the passionately held convictions of Eric Mascall, on the one hand, and Gerd Theissen, on the other. Each believes that the kind of approach represented by the other constitutes a kind of moral *betrayal* of authentic theological scholarship. Mascall writes, 'We have been so anxious to be accepted as intellectually respectable in our modern secularized universities . . . that we have taken for granted the desupernaturalization of Jesus and have substituted the study of early Christian psychology for the study of divine revelation.'[10] Theissen comments, 'There can be no recourse to privileged knowledge or authorities . . . I shall ignore the view that it is possible to have privileged access to the truth. Instead of this I shall look for technical competence . . . There can be no question of defending religion in its traditional form.'[11]

A diagnosis of some causes of the problem and a way forward

Why is such a divergent range of standpoints represented in the debate, and why has the debate so often led to bitterness and misunderstanding? We have already suggested that too often it is forgotten, or has never been understood, that there are *moral* constraints and pressures from *both* sides of the traditional arguments. Too often the debate has been misconstrued as a *moral* issue of honesty or academic integrity on one side, and as a *religious* matter of faithfulness to authoritative doctrine on the other. But such a way of construing the issue leaves much out of account. Even worse, it invites one side to see themselves as martyrs in the cause of honesty and the other side to see themselves as martyrs in the cause of theological faithfulness.

Membership of the academic community does indeed carry with it certain moral obligations. Each academic discipline evolves certain 'rules of the game', and a scholar has a moral obligation either to play by these rules or at least to offer rigorous rational justification for calling the rules in question. Knowledge of 'the rules' on the part of the teacher and student is part of what we think of as 'professional' competence in the area. Like a good referee, while a scholar may have a strong personal preference about which side wins in a particular game, the moral rules of scholarship dictate that he gives each side their maximum opportunity to win, within the rules. Scholarly integrity, according to the philosopher Alan Montefiore, involves helping or hindering either side 'in completely equal measure with respect to his application of the rules of the game . . . It is a matter of complete indifference to him *qua* referee whether it is one side or the other that has incurred a penalty. It is true that in imposing a penalty he is hindering the offending side and helping its opponents, but *he would have behaved in exactly the same way had their positions been reversed.'*[12] Whatever his *personal* desires, he has a professional *role* that imposes the moral constraint of fairness in handling evidence and arguments, akin to that of a judge in the courtroom or a referee in the field. To confuse *neutrality*, or lack of it, with *impartiality*, or lack of it, would be to betray the moral trust placed in him by the university, his academic peers and his students.

Nevertheless, this very disjunction, or at least distinction, between person and role has implications for the other side of the debate. For very often the Christian scholar performs not only the role of a member of the academic community, but also the role of a teacher or minister of the Church. This role, too, is one which carries with it the privilege of trust on the part of others, and this, too, carries with it its own *moral* obligations. Those who look to their Christian pastors and teachers for spiritual nourishment and for edification of faith cannot but feel a sense of moral betrayal if or when these very teachers seem to undermine aspects of the corporate witness of the believing community. The Church no less than the academic community, has 'rules' by which it lives and hands on its spiritual resources.

The more closely we look at the problems and issues, the more clearly we see the moral complexity of constraints which are experienced on all sides. The scholar who works

himself to work exclusively within the dictates imposed by a single model, regardless of the demands of the particular theological task in hand. If he sees himself as wearing the mantle of the Enlightenment critic, he will be inclined to adopt an attitude of suspicion and scepticism towards religious tradition. If, on the other hand, he sees himself only as shepherd and guardian of the flock, he may become almost obsessively paranoid about 'dangers' and 'threats' in theological teaching and research. The Christian scholar who is historically sensitive to the functions and limitations of all these adopted roles, however, will refrain from assigning some overarching model to his own scholarly activity in advance of knowing the nature of the specific theological task in hand. There are times when the urgent task is to move discussion forward beyond tired arguments and well-worn grooves; and there are times when it is more appropriate to issue a prophetic summons to renewed faithfulness.

It is instructive to note, however, that once again this principle is not exclusive to Christian theology. A considerable amount of research has been carried out in the area of educational psychology on the nature of creativity in the school and in the university. What emerges most clearly is that creative thinking is not to be equated simply with sheer novelty. It is true that creative scholarship entails individual insight, individual critical judgement, and above all a dimension of willingness to engage in risk. This is why, to return to D. M. MacKinnon's essay, 'the university teacher of theology must be a man at once committed and uncommitted . . . He must be prepared to find the outcome of his work totally other than his hopes and anticipations.'[13] Nevertheless individualist criticism and novelty is creative rather than merely eccentric and destructive only when it performs a productive and constructive function in relation to the wider tradition *within* which the novelty or criticism means anything significant. In terms of the psychology of education, creativity depends on *interaction between* the

31

convergent-type thinking which characterizes the tradition of the community and the divergent-type thinking of the individual. A number of writers urge that 'creativity arises out of conventional intelligence . . . Creative thinking occurs when the boundaries of the known are first mastered through convergent processes, and then extended, by the application of divergent processes.'[14]

In a less obvious and less direct way this principle may be said to operate even in some schools of modern art, where the 'commonsense' plain man may be tempted to feel that the distinction between creativity and arbitrary novelty is no longer possible. Creativity in some schools of art depends on what Merleau-Ponty calls the principle of 'coherent deformation'. The familiar is skewed and presented from a strikingly unusual physical or imaginative angle, in such a way that it is seen in an entirely fresh light. But if it is not the *familiar* which is re-presented in this way, the whole exercise loses its point as a creative presentation, and becomes mere fantasy or self-indulgence on the part of the artist.

In the event, then, the Christian scholar who is entirely dominated by the model of himself as pioneer, explorer, or Enlightenment critic, is less likely to contribute genuinely creative work than the Christian scholar who adopts a plurality of models which allow room for the constraints of tradition, or for what is 'familiar' from the standpoint of the whole Christian community. The particular complexity and delicacy of the debate about academic freedom arises, however, from the fact that the post-Enlightenment scholar stands in a multiplicity of traditions. The 'familiar' in the tradition of the Church is no longer the same as the 'familiar' in the history of the academic discipline within which he works. What constitutes convergent thinking within the context of the academic community is not the same as what constitutes convergent thinking in the context of the Church. Here we reach the heart of the matter. Any genuinely creative thinker works from within a given context. And the constraints and tensions experienced by the Christian scholar arise from the duality, or more correctly, multiplicity of contexts or traditions, within which he works.

The force of some standard arguments on both sides of the debate

We have space only to select some of the standard arguments which are put forward from both sides of the debate. First, we look at those which are offered as a defence of the importance of academic freedom as a necessary context for theological teaching and research.

1   The customary starting point concerns the importance of intellectual honesty and integrity. Bultmann cites this quality as the most important positive feature of theological liberalism, although he allows that it also seduced liberal scholars into a naively optimistic and objectivist view of the task of historical research, especially in relation to the figure of Jesus. He speaks of 'the development of *the critical sense*, . . . freedom and veracity . . . the earnest search for radical truth'. He recalls his sense of gratitude as a student to G. Krüger's insistence that theology was 'unchurchly': 'He saw the task of theology to be to imperil souls, to lead man into doubt, to shatter all credulity. Here, we felt, was the atmosphere of truth in which alone we could breathe.'[15] Bultmann contrasts this with the atmosphere of intellectual compromise which as a student he believed characterized the orthodox university theology of the day. That Bultmann overpresses his point is clear from the fact that he feels obliged to offer a peculiar kind of theological defence of this approach. The Pauline doctrine of justification by grace alone is applied as a theory of knowledge, as if to suggest that intellectual defence of the Christian faith constitutes a kind of self-justification by intellectual 'works'. By this means Bultmann can solve the problem of academic

freedom and the morality of Christian scholarship in a highly distinctive way, making a virtue out of the post-Enlightenment necessity of scepticism and doubt. But intellectual honesty and integrity is not the exclusive preserve of liberalism or radicalism. The fundamental importance of intellectual honesty is wholly correct; but the liberalism which Bultmann describes merely oversimplifies a complex moral problem by placing the doubts of the individual scholar at the top of a descending hierarchy, regardless of what the actual issue under discussion happens to be.

2   Even though Bultmann's particular use of the doctrine of justification by grace is open to question, it nevertheless remains true that to argue for the place of theology in the setting of academic freedom within the university reflects certain basic insights of the Reformation. Indeed this point was raised in the controversy surrounding Gesenius and the University of Halle to which we have already referred. Gerhard Ebeling and Jaroslav Pelikan are among those who insist that Martin Luther saw himself first and foremost as a university professor of Old Testament, standing in the tradition of humanistic scholarship. Scripture must be allowed to speak in such a way that it may correct and reform the life of the Church; but if it is taught and studied only by those who already see everything through the eyes of that life, how can the Bible speak freely and powerfully to the Church's condition, confronting even churchman as a word of both grace and judgement? For this reason, Pelikan observes, the Bible and theology are 'too important a part of scholarly enquiry to be left only to churchly theologians'.[16] In other words, it is to the good of the *Church* that the Bible is not studied and taught exclusively by the official spokesmen of the Church of the day. Otherwise there is the danger that the Church will hear only what it wishes to hear. Thus Ebeling asserts that Luther received his certainty of vocation 'from the sober fact of his academic calling, which gave him the right and the duty to speak, even

against his monastic vows and his duty of obedience to the
hierarchy and the Church: "I have often said, and say again,
I will not exchange my professorship for anything in the
world".'[17] T. F. Torrance considers that in this respect the
Reformers raised the question of objectivity in theological method. The Reformation, he argues, sprang from 'a
repentant readiness to rethink all preconceptions and
presuppositions, to put all traditional ideas to the test face
to face with the object'.[18]

3 It follows from all this that theology can never be
confined to the ghetto of one particular tradition or
segment of life. Perhaps no one makes this point more
cogently than Wolfhart Pannenberg, who is also thoroughly
aware of the subjective dimension of human understanding.
Pannenberg points out that the concern about the scientific
status of theology in the university has been bound up
since the twelfth or thirteenth century with the desire 'to
defend Christianity by generally accepted criteria . . . If
theology were now forced to disappear from universities on
the grounds maintained by many people, that it is essentially
tied to authority and therefore unscientific, this would be
a severe setback for the Christian understanding of
truth.'[19] In one of his earlier essays Pannenberg speaks of
'the intellectual obligation that goes along with the use of
the word "God".' 'Because God is the creator of all things, it
belongs to the task of theology to understand all being in
relation to God.'[20] The target of Pannenberg's criticisms is
especially those Protestant theologians, who, following the
disintegration of the naive historical objectivism of liberalism, sought to locate Christian truth wholly in the realm of
the subjective or existential. W. W. Bartley has traced the
course of this trend under the suggestive title *The Retreat to
Commitment*, published in 1962. Paul Tillich, with his notion
of ultimate concern, comes under attack no less sharply
than theologians in the Barthian tradition. In particular the
argument that we cannot escape a ghetto theology since

'everything depends on one's presuppositions' is dismissed as a *rational* excuse for *irrational* commitment.

4   A number of pragmatic arguments have been put forward for the importance of academic freedom in theology. A genuine openness to revise conclusions, for example, may seem less defensive, self-centred, or even arrogant, than a dogmatism which cannot tolerate any challenge. More to the point, defensive dogmatism has almost always had unproductive historical consequences. It is also worth noting the warning offered by Ebeling in his recent essay on the place of the Bible in the university. He points out that if Christian theologians withdraw, or are forced to withdraw, from the university, those from non-theological disciplines will be left to fend for themselves in their own study of the Bible. Many disciplines, he observes, have continuous encounters with the Bible: whether we think of classical studies, English literature, social history, or the history of ideas. 'The loss would not be that the Bible would no longer be available, but that the university would be left alone with it.'[21] It would be possible to cite other arguments which have been put forward in the debate, but we have selected, by way of example, those which seem to be most important.

The other side of the debate, however, also offers its standard arguments, and some of these also invite a measure of reappraisal in the light of the earlier part of our discussion. They can perhaps be stated rather more briefly.

1   The major cause of unhappiness about theology in the context of the university is that it loses its character as proclamation, confession, witness and worship. Instead it seems to become reduced to the level of a merely empirical or phenomenological study. This problem is also bound up with the different methodological approaches of biblical studies and systematic or doctrinal theology. The rise and development of biblical criticism rightly called attention to

the importance of using methods of linguistic, literary, and historical research which are not peculiar to Christian theology, and the effectiveness or validity of which have been proved or tested in other disciplines. But from the point of view of the believing Christian community, the study of the Bible also involves more than this, even if it does not involve less than this. So dominant have the empirical aspects become that Eric Mascall complains: 'The study of God and of his revelation of himself to man in Jesus Christ has been overshadowed, and indeed effectively superseded, by the various disciplines which in the past were held to be ancillary to it . . . Theology, having lost its unifying factor . . . has fallen apart into a number of disparate activities . . .'[22] Mascall lays the blame for this largely on attempts to make theology 'respectable in the context of a virtually secularized university'.

2   The trans-empirical dimension of theology is further underlined by the part played by understanding, judgement, and decision in theological argument, especially in the context of the transmission and criticism of tradition. The work of Bernard Lonergan, among others, serves to call attention to this point. Indeed Lonergan forcefully reminds us that the grave limitations of empirical or merely descriptive methods are seen in the human sciences in general no less than in theology.[23] The philosopher Stuart Hampshire puts his finger on the point when he observes: 'The really difficult issue of commitment and of the morality of scholarship, is this: how are we to decide what questions are worth asking, what problems are worth raising, or, more strongly, what problems must be raised?'[24] A university course in biblical studies, for example, would certainly raise questions about the Exile. It would ask why *Israel* saw the Exile as an act of God, but would be much less likely to ask whether the Exile *was* an act of God, since the answer could not be given in terms of generally accepted criteria. Thus, from a confessional or church viewpoint, a

university syllabus in biblical studies often chooses to omit some quite fundamental questions in the name of objectivity. The Church might even claim that the university course was unduly *narrow*.

3 The third major argument of those who are anxious about unrestrained freedom for the Christian scholar concerns his moral and theological obligations to the Christian community of which he is part. His Christian confession carries obligations with it, and these are still more pronounced if the scholar in question is also the holder of some Christian office, to whom others look with trust for guidance. We have already said that part of the tension experienced by many Christian scholars is due to their recognition of two quite distinct sets of obligations to the academic community and to the Christian community, both of which have given them privileges which also lay responsibilities upon them. If a scholar who belongs to both communities acts or thinks in unscholarly or in unchristian ways, he risks perplexing outsiders who begin to doubt the credibility of the community, and he risks betraying the trust of the community.

4 The whole notion of 'guarding the faith' has become unfashionable today, especially since western society, partly in reaction against Marxism and all forms of totalitarianism, prizes tolerance, good humour, freedom, and a pluralism of 'viewpoints' almost above every other virtue. Certainly when we compare the attitude of the early church Fathers and the later parts of the New Testament towards the rule of faith and tradition, we move into a different world of values. One unfortunate result of this is that many Protestants have retreated so far from the notion of a succession of faith or doctrine that the entire weight of the idea of succession is left to rest on more Catholic ideas concerning ecclesiastical institution. One small movement in Anglicanism which attempts slightly to

redress the balance, however, is the very recent report of the Church of England Doctrine Commission, *Believing in the Church*. There, John Bowker points out, for example, that the Church performs the necessary function of a 'system' in systems-theory, of preserving the continuity and identity of the community's spiritual resource. He shows further, that certain boundary-markers must be operative if this continuity is to be maintained in an effective and recognizable way. In my own essay in the Report I have tried to argue for these principles in the area of the theory of knowledge, showing that the growth and criticism of knowledge rest on the corporate memory of the community and its tradition, no less than on individual enquiry. When he spoke of freedom of conscience, Luther spoke as one whose conscience was captive to the word of God, and not as the individual of Enlightenment rationalism.[25]

Tradition, community, and the debate about fact and value

It is clear that the standard arguments on both sides of the debate carry weight, and that either side can be ignored only at the price of gross oversimplification. The Christian scholar is subject to at least two distinct sets of moral constraints, deriving on the one hand from the standards demanded by the academic community, and on the other hand from those which belong to the Christian community and the gospel which it represents.

In the light of what we have already said about the diversity of *roles* adopted by the Christian scholar it is tempting to think that the answer to our problem is for him to follow the imperatives dictated by the given roles assigned by each community in given situations. But the scholar is not simply a collection of separate role-performances; he is a single responsible thinking human being. He cannot, as F. F. Bruce's reflections remind us, be one person in the pulpit and an entirely different person in the lecture-room. At least, he cannot be two different people with moral integrity, even though in actual practice a sensitive Christian scholar will assess what it is appropriate to say or not to say, in the light of the needs and conventions which belong to each particular situation.

If we compare the constraints experienced by the theological scholar with those felt by his counterpart in political theory or the social sciences, we may see that further light is shed on his problem by the debate about value-free knowledge and the role of 'tradition', or the communal foundations of enquiry, action and criticism. It is a mistake to assume that if only he could free himself from the constraints of 'church' theology the Christian scholar would be liberated simply to follow 'the facts'. In none of the humanities (whatever might be claimed for the physical sciences) is it possible to achieve a totally clear-cut disjunction between 'facts' and values. This lesson is underlined, in particular by several writers in political theory. For example, in an essay entitled 'Neutrality in Political Science', Charles Taylor discusses the status of such facts as the number of French workers who vote Communist, or the number of Americans who vote Republican. No one disputes that such statistics constitute genuine facts. However, it is a matter of scholarly *judgement* what particular facts and statistics are selected from an almost infinite number of situations or events, and within what frame of reference they are placed in order to formulate explanatory hypotheses concerning their significance.

After examining several examples of facts and their evaluation, Taylor concludes: 'The non-neutrality of the theoretical findings of political science need not surprise us. In setting out a given framework, a theorist is also setting out the gamut of possible polities and policies.'[26] Any coherent attempt to arrive at explanation or significance entails an interaction between factual findings and some value position.

In the debate about the morality of Christian scholarship,

40

each of the two opposite sides has been tempted to overstress fact or value, whereas a more balanced approach would take account of the interaction between the two. Sometimes academic theologians in the tradition of liberal Protestantism have stressed the work of the lone individual scholar dealing with 'the facts', as if the key to his success was simply to emancipate him from the chains of a dogmatic tradition. On the other side, theology is withdrawn into the protective ghetto of the Christian community on the grounds that only the framework of the tradition can determine what counts as a fact and what constitutes its meaning, as if a fact such as that of the rise of Easter faith could never stand on its own feet and speak for itself at the bar of general enquiry.

In practice, the debate among such thinkers as Schutz, Kuhn and Popper has shown that *both* poles of this dialectic must be taken fully into account. Alfred Schutz, among others, has rightly shown that all meaning results from interpretation; that meaning is constructed, not simply discovered, and that the typifications through which a community perceives reality have their place in shaping how that meaning is constructed.[27] For this reason, hermeneutics has become increasingly important in the social sciences, no less than in theology and in biblical studies.[28] Thomas Kuhn has convincingly shown us the important part played by controlling models, or paradigms, within the scholarly community. Until they are modified, or until others take their place, they make certain ways of setting out problems more easy to arrive at than others, and they tend to suggest the kind of solution that will most readily count as an answer.[29] Nevertheless, the standard counter-arguments of Karl Popper and others remain equally valid. The paradigms do no more than suggest, rather than dictate, the course of subsequent debate and their adequacy can be tested alongside that of other paradigms by a rational process of trial and error.[30]

A balanced account of the morality of Christian scholarship will try to hold all these insights together. On one side, Popper's insistence on the universality of rational criteria must be respected. Theological arguments and conclusions must be submitted to testing outside the protective confines of some Christian intellectual ghetto. Theology must take its place alongside other disciplines, and be studied in an atmosphere of academic freedom. But the insistence of Kuhn and Schutz on the importance of the community must also be given due weight. *If it fails to submit its formulations to testing outside its own tradition, the Christian community risks the loss of its claims to rationality and universality. But equally, if it shows inadequate concern for the preservation of its tradition, it risks the loss of its continuity and recognizable identity.* The Christian scholar takes up his position between the two sets of constraints imposed by these considerations.

Traditionally it might have been said that Roman Catholic theology was more concerned with the maintenance of tradition, and Protestant theology was more concerned with its criticism. But the situation is no longer so straightforward, even if it ever was so. On one side, Barthian theology stands as a witness to the inadequacy of the liberal tradition in Protestant theology, and it is especially Barthian theologians such as Hermann Diem and others who most strongly stress the status of Christian theology as that which is done within the Christian community. As confession, as testimony, and as doxology, it belongs to the realm of value and not merely fact. Such an outlook might be said to stand in contrast to the traditional Thomist emphasis on natural theology. On the other side, the Second Vatican Council has shown a striking concern for freedom of enquiry. One of its documents urges, for example, that all higher education should be undertaken 'with a true liberty of scientific enquiry'.[31] Indeed while many official Catholic pronouncements urge the importance of tradition, an increasingly wide range of attitudes seems to be emerging towards the questions which have been under discussion among individual Catholic scholars, especially in biblical studies.

We conclude, then, that the Christian scholar has to live with the tensions and pressures which arise from a plurality of moral constraints and obligations. Perhaps, as D. M. MacKinnon has argued, for many Christian scholars (although by their own testimony not for all) an experience of pressure and painful struggle is a sign of authentic vocation and discipleship. Certainly there is no abstract, generalizing, sweeping solution to the problem. In his discussion of the morality of scholarship in philosophy and the social sciences, Stuart Hampshire offers the scholar one consolation for this. He points out that the experience of being drawn in more than one direction, the experience of wanting to say 'Yes' to more than one path of argument, is precisely what gives *vitality* to scholarship.[32] The task of wrestling with resisting *complex* material is what gives the scholarly mind its edge and stimulates the scholar's imagination. If this is so, a recognition of the complexities of our subject and of the need to say 'Yes' to both sides of its main arguments will serve the Christian scholar better than some simplistic but one-sided attempt to offer any over-easy solution.

NOTES

1 Max Black, ed., *The Morality of Scholarship*. Cornell University Press, New York, 1967.

2 F. F. Bruce, *In Retrospect. Remembrance of Things Past* (Pickering and Inglis, London, 1980), pp. 143-4.

3 ibid., p. 143.

4 Donald MacKinnon, 'Theology as a Discipline of a Modern University', in T. Shanin, ed., *The Rules of the Game. Cross-Disciplinary Essays on Models in Scholarly Thought* (Tavistock Publications, London, 1972), p. 170.

5 ibid., p. 172; cf. pp. 164-78.

6 G. R. Evans, *Old Arts and New Technology. The Beginnings of Theology as an Academic Discipline* (Clarendon Press, Oxford, 1980), p. 57 and *passim*.

7   Wolfhart Pannenberg, *Theology and the Philosophy of Science* (Westminster Press, Philadelphia, and Darton, Longman and Todd, London, 1976), p. 13.

8   *Doctrine in the Church of England. The Report of the Commission on Christian Doctrine Appointed by the Archbishops of Canterbury and York in 1922* (SPCK, London, 1938), pp. 36–9; and *Believing in the Church. The Corporate Nature of Faith*, A Report by the Doctrine Commission of the Church of England (SPCK, London, 1981), especially pp. 129–34.

9   *Believing in the Church*, p. 296.

10 E. L. Mascall, *Theology and the Gospel of Christ. An Essay in Reorientation* (SPCK, London, 1977), p. 1.

11 Gerd Theissen, *On Having a Critical Faith* (SCM, London, 1979), pp. 10–11.

12 Alan Montefiore, ed., *Neutrality and Impartiality. The University and Political Commitment* (Cambridge University Press 1975), p. 9 (my italics).

13 D. M. MacKinnon, 'Theology as a Discipline of a Modern University', loc. cit., p. 168.

14 A. J. Cropley, *Creativity* (Longmans, London, 1967), p. 29. Cf. H. E. Gruber and G. Terrell, ed., *Contemporary Approaches to Creative Thinking* (Atherton Press, New York, 1962), especially J. S. Bruner's essay, 'The Creative Surprise'; and C. W. Taylor, ed., *Creativity: Progress and Potential* (McGraw-Hill, New York, 1964).

15 R. Bultmann, *Faith and Understanding. Collected Essays* (E. tr. SCM, London, 1969) pp. 29–30.

16 J. Pelikan, *The Christian Intellectual* (Collins, London, 1966), p. 103.

17 G. Ebeling, *Luther. An Introduction to his Thought* (E. tr. Collins, London, 1972), p. 17.

18 T. F. Torrance, *Theological Science* (Oxford University Press, 1969), p. 75.

19 W. Pannenberg, *Theology and the Philosophy of Science*, p. 13.

20 W. Pannenberg, *Basic Questions in Theology*, vol. i (E. tr. SCM, London, 1970) p. 1.

21 Gerhard Ebeling, 'The Bible as a Document of the University', in Hans Dieter Betz, ed., *The Bible as a Document of the University* (Scholars Press, Chico, 1981), p. 14. Cf. also G. Ebeling, *The Study of Theology* (E. tr. Collins, London, 1979), pp. 81–94.

22   E. L. Mascall, *Theology and the Gospel of Christ*, p. 22.

23   Bernard J. F. Lonergan, *Method in Theology* (Darton, Longman, and Todd, London, 1972), pp. 248–9 and *passim*.

24   S. Hampshire, in *The Morality of Scholarship*, p. 40.

25   *Believing in the Church*, pp. 45–78 and 159–89.

26   Charles Taylor, 'Neutrality in Political Science', in Peter Laslett and W. G. Runciman, ed., *Philosophy, Politics, and Society*. Third Series (Blackwell, Oxford, 1967), p. 55; pp. 25–57.

27   Alfred Schutz, *Collected Papers* (3 vols. Nijhoff, The Hague, 1962–6). Cf. also R. R. Cox, *Schutz's Theory of Relevance* (Nijhoff, The Hague, 1978), pp. 1–32.

28   Cf. Zygmunt Bauman, *Hermeneutics and Social Science* (Hutchinson, London, 1978); and A. C. Thiselton, *The Two Horizons* (Paternoster, Exeter, 1980).

29   Thomas S. Kuhn, *The Structure of Scientific Revolution*. 2nd edn University of Chicago Press 1970.

30   Karl Popper, 'Normal Science and its Dangers', in I. Lakatos and A. Musgrave, ed., *Criticism and the Growth of Knowledge* (Cambridge University Press 1970), pp. 51–8.

31   Vatican II, *Gravissimum educationis* (28 October 1965), sect. 10.

32   S. Hampshire, 'Commitment and Imagination', in Max Black, ed., *The Morality of Scholarship*, pp. 42–3.

3
The ARCIC Statements in the Context of Other Dialogues

Mary Tanner

An impressive but complex activity of theological dialogue has gathered momentum in the last few years. The work of the Anglican–Roman Catholic International Commission is one example.[1] A–L, A–RC, A–O, A–RCusa, B–R, L–R, L–Rusa, M–RC, M–RCaus, O–Rnaus, Ps–RC, R–RC etc . . . are just a few of the new algebraic signs creeping into the ecumenical language of the eighties, as baffling to an outsider as the old Pentateuchal signs of the beginning of the century. These bilateral dialogues, on an international, national or regional level, between Churches and confessional families, form an intricate network of involvement giving rise to a new and complex set of relationships between the churches. Any one Church may be engaged at any one time at different levels with a variety of partners. The doctrinal statements resulting from these dialogues are an important part, though only one part, of the journey towards unity. They provide a marvellous assurance that in the face of bitter quarrels and deep divisions of the past many Churches today are discovering together new understandings which transcend inherited polarized positions and which challenge them to seek for closer partnership in life and mission.

The welcome involvement of the Roman Catholic Church,

resulting from the Second Vatican Council, has increased dramatically the number of bilateral dialogues. But the work of reaching doctrinal agreement already had a lengthy history in the multilateral dialogues of regional and national councils of Churches and in the various union negotiation schemes. Of particular importance in setting the scene for assessing the work of ARCIC is the work of the World Council of Churches in which, together with Orthodox and Protestant partners, the Anglican and Roman Catholic Churches have been involved, through their membership of the Faith and Order Commission. Attempts to reach doctrinal agreement stretch as far back as the First World Conference in Lausanne, 1927. At this early stage the work of the multilaterals was largely descriptive, concerned with pointing out fundamental agreements on the one hand and the deep points of division and disagreement on the other. It is hard to overestimate the importance of Lausanne in the growing awareness of each other's traditions and the establishing of a commitment to engage in theological discussion in the search for unity. It was the subjects of that particular agenda, the nature of the Church, the common confession of faith, sacraments and ministry, that have continued to be the focal points of theological debate in the ever growing number of dialogues.

While the descriptive work of Lausanne led to greater understanding and respect, it was not sufficient to move the Churches closer together. A turning point in the work of the Commission came with the focusing of attention on the search for a consensus which might be recognized as sufficient for the Churches to live in full visible unity. In 1974 three Agreed Statements on Baptism, Eucharist and Ministry were published, bringing together the fruits of the discussions that had taken place since Lausanne.[2] The texts were encouraging, for they demonstrated a growing convergence in a wide ecumenical context, particularly in the areas of baptism and Eucharist, but also showed

47

significant shifts in the understanding of ministry. Important too was the beginning of a new process of theological response. Churches were invited to send back comments to Geneva showing how far the statements were consonant with their own beliefs. In this way statements which illustrated agreement by a group of theologians moved in the direction of being statements agreed by the Churches. Careful analysis of the responses led to the production of revised texts to be published in 1982. In these new texts the convergence process has moved further forward. What can be said together forms the main text and the points at which disagreement remains are discussed in commentary form. These texts provide a valuable frame of reference for studying any one of the bilateral statements including the ARCIC texts on the Eucharist and ministry. They help the partners in a bilateral discussion to see their own conclusions within the perspective of what has emerged as the consensus of all the Churches. There are many things in these statements which would have been unimaginable a few years ago and they are surely signs of hope in a period of some tension and despondency in the ecumenical movement.

In assessing the achievements of ARCIC in the light of other dialogues it has to be remembered that each set of bilateral texts is related to a very particular context of past division and is directed towards the achievement of different ends within the one movement towards unity. The texts vary greatly and we are never comparing like with like. The Methodist–Roman Catholic conversations, for example, have a particular character precisely because the Methodist Churches did not have their origins in a direct break with the Roman Catholic Church. The aims of the conversations were to move towards a deeper mutual understanding and a possible convergence, to secure better relationships between the two communions, and to make more effective their co-operative work in many parts of the world. The question of unity in one form or another was never a stated aim. With the Lutheran–Roman Catholic conversations, on the other hand, the history of the division of the sixteenth century determined to a large extent the agenda, and the expressed aim was much more specific than the Methodist–Roman Catholic dialogue. It was a search for a theological consensus 'sufficiently broad and solid to provide a basis for a qualified mutual recognition and occasional reciprocal intercommunion'. The Anglican–Roman Catholic dialogue worked in quite another historical and theological context, giving rise to its particular agenda and characteristic documents. It brought together two episcopal Churches with their own painful history of division stemming from the Reformation, with its scars and still open wounds, but also the many contemporary signs of hope in life and work. The Bull *Apostolicae Curae* of 1896, in which Leo XIII declared Anglican orders to be 'absolutely null and utterly void' was inevitably important background when the Commission decided to concentrate upon ministry as one of its subjects. At the outset the intention was of working towards organic unity of the two Churches but as the discussions have progressed emphasis has been placed more on the notion of unity by stages. This is important, for it means that the statements themselves can be viewed as a stage in the movement or process towards unity. Further it helps us to see that the goal of organic unity, impossible to describe in any blueprint, unfolds at each stage of the journey.

The bilateral statements vary enormously, ranging from the discursive style of the Methodist–Roman Catholic dialogue to the tightly packed, closely argued texts of ARCIC. These texts include Eucharistic Doctrine (Windsor 1971), Ministry and Ordination (Canterbury 1973), Authority in the Church I and II (Venice 1976 and Windsor 1981). The closely argued texts bring with them their own particular problems. The Windsor text on the Eucharist, for example, comprises only twelve brief paragraphs, behind which lies a lengthy history of controversy. It is helpful to recall that 'the Commission was not asked to produce a comprehensive treatise on the Eucharist, but to examine differences which in the controversies of the past divided our two communions'. Nevertheless it is often precisely because the texts are so condensed, so kept to a minimum, that questions have had to be asked. It is all too easy for those involved in the dialogue, in an attempt to avoid divisive language of the past, to develop a special style of their own which articulates to the participants the understanding they have reached together but which is far from comprehensible to those who have not gone through a similar process and are not convinced of the need to let go of inherited language. Inevitably there has been a genuine uneasiness about whether agreement is more apparent than real in the short ARCIC texts. This is not to question the integrity of those involved, but to point to a very real problem in assessing texts of this genre without access to the lengthy discussions which lie behind them. It is here that the 'Elucidations' have a very important part to play and they must now be read alongside the texts.[3] They go a long way to providing a necessary explanation of areas in which genuine difficulties have been encountered, showing how important it is for the churches to enter into dialogue with a statement in the convergence to consensus process.

The Windsor statement on the Eucharist was the first of the ARCIC texts to be published, in 1971. Together with the subsequent Elucidations (and the two must be taken together) it witnesses to a remarkable degree of convergence, particularly in two areas, the doctrine of the real presence and the understanding of sacrifice. On the subject of the real presence many of the bilateral texts agree with Windsor in affirming the real presence of the risen Christ in the Eucharist, although there are marked differences of emphasis. The consensus has been easier to state negatively than positively, and has emerged partly through the avoidance of two extreme positions, on the one hand, a particular philosophical interpretation of transubstantiation, on the other a reduction of the presence to a commemoration of an event firmly tied to the past. The bilaterals connect the presence with the entire eucharistic action but acknowledge a special connection between the elements and the presence. This is described in most statements in 'sign' language. It is precisely at this point that the Windsor statement is stronger.

> Communion with Christ in the eucharist presupposes his true presence, effectually signified by the bread and wine which, in this mystery, become his body and blood.

Just how the bread and wine become his body and blood is not stated. The weight of the text is indeed on the reality of the presence and not on the notion of how change takes place. Nevertheless the word 'become' in the Windsor text appears to go beyond other bilaterals and is taken by some to imply a materialistic conception of Christ's presence. Although the emotive word 'transubstantiation' is avoided in the text, its appearance in a footnote serves to compound the confusion, as does the use of the word 'change'.

> The term (transubstantiation) should be seen as affirming the *fact* of Christ's presence and of the mysterious and radical change which takes place.

In responding to the disquiet felt by the words 'become' and 'change', the Elucidation points out that they must not be taken out of the context of the Windsor text as a whole, where Christ's presence in the elements is neither divided from the encounter in the whole eucharistic celebration nor from the action of the Holy Spirit. It goes further in helping us grasp what was intended by the use of 'become'. It does this by stating clearly four things that were not intended. It is of course easier to say what is *not* intended than to be clear about what is intended. It seems that 'become' must only be understood within the concept of 'sacramental order': that is, that order in which the 'realities of faith' become present in visible and tangible signs of the earthly order, and in faith the Christian apprehends and encounters Christ present in those signs. It is in the sphere of sacramental order that we are able to distinguish between two sacramental actions within the framework of the whole Eucharist: two actions which are inextricably bound together. The first is the moment when the Lord offers himself gratuitously and it is this initiative of God which is all-absorbing, and the second is when we approach in faith to accept this gift in communion. Here one focus is on the fact that Christ is really present in the eucharistic elements after the consecration and the other is on the fact that when those consecrated elements are given and received, the believing recipient is indeed nourished by Christ. These two elements represent two understandings of the Eucharist which have been separately and almost exclusively emphasized, both claiming their own adherents. What the Elucidation says is that both consecration and reception must be kept together in a complementary way within one understanding of sacramental reality and only then can the word 'become' in the Windsor text be understood. Many will welcome a new clarity emerging here in an area of old division. The agreement reached here goes significantly beyond that arrived at in other bilaterals, and the World Council text remains descriptive of differing positions at this point.

What is believed about the relation between the presence of Christ and the elements finds its outward expression in the devotional practices of our Churches. Here differences are to be found as much within Anglicanism as between our two Churches. Although Windsor had nothing to say about reservation or veneration it was taken up in the Elucidation, where both are understood as an extension of the Eucharist. Without a firm linkage there is distortion. Even so, for some, veneration will clearly never be acceptable, for it appears to prevent the holding together of the two foci of sacramental reality, that of God's gift of himself and the reception by the faithful. Any form of veneration will be taken to imply the former and exclude the latter. ARCIC's conclusion, however, is that it is possible to accept both the diverse theological judgement at this point and a plurality of practice without a denial of the underlying common doctrinal agreement. This is an important conclusion, for what emerges is what legitimate diversity might mean within a united Church.

A second highly divisive issue in the past has been the understanding of the Eucharist as sacrifice. Here again remarkable convergence is appearing, not only between Anglicans and Roman Catholics, but in the wider ecumenical scene, as the World Council text illustrates. As in the Windsor Statement, a common starting point is the emphatic assertion that the sacrifice of Christ was once for all: there can be no repetition. There is also agreement that the sacrifice of Christ is effectively present in the whole eucharistic celebration. It has been the biblical concept of memorial (*anamnesis*) which has been the important concept whereby this has become acceptable. Catholic sacrificialists and reformed non-sacrificialists have been drawn together in a new understanding of *anamnesis*. In the Eucharist we recall the sacrifice of Christ in a dynamic way that puts us in touch with the saving act of God. In and through the proclamation of the once occurring sacrifice, the effects which are eternal are experienced anew and become effective through the power of the Spirit. In this sense the once-for-all sacrifice is made present. The term 'to make present' must not be understood as belonging to our category of linear time, but, as the Elucidation suggests, belongs to 'sacramental reality'. In worship, linear time ceases to be a primary category as past, present and future are drawn together. It would be nonsense to say Calvary recurred. On the other hand to say that it is made present does justice to the experience of many Christians.

In their preface the co-chairmen say that nothing essential has been omitted. While this seems right there is nevertheless one important dimension which, by comparison with the World Council text, is absent, namely the relation between the Eucharist and the world. The Eucharist is not simply the meal of the faithful in which Anglicans and Roman Catholics long one day to share freely, it is also the feast where the Church may recognize the signs of renewal already at work in the world, and where, united with Christ in a special way, it prays for the world and is the centre from which we go out renewed by the Spirit to act as reconcilers in a broken world. Such a concern for the world is not an optional extra in our understanding of the Eucharist but is integral and deserves to be expressed in the eucharistic agreement between our churches.

There is indeed a remarkable consensus emerging on the doctrine of the Eucharist amongst the different traditions in the ecumenical movement. A common language is developing which allows churches to recognize valid elements in each others' traditions. In the light of the bitter controversies of the past it is astonishing that such a measure of agreement is emerging. Constructive discussion has been possible because of the general climate of ecumenical relations, the new insights we all share in biblical criticism and church history, and a willingness to go back together behind the points of division to foundations and to be open to new insights discovered there. Equally significant in relation to the Eucharist is the growing recognition of the centrality of the Eucharist in the lives of many churches and the growth in what can only be described as a eucharistic consciousness. It is this which enables the notion of 'sacramental reality' to be understood, a notion which plays such an important part in the ARCIC discussions. Taken together, the Windsor statement and its Elucidation mark a greater degree of convergence than found elsewhere – surely enough to confirm the members of ARCIC in the opinion that it is indeed 'substantial agreement', such that the doctrine of the Eucharist can no longer constitute an obstacle in the movement of our two Churches towards unity.

Like the Eucharist, ministry has been one of the major topics in the bilateral conversations, though the points emphasized differ according to whether the Churches are episcopally ordered or not. There is general agreement in the statements that the only context for understanding ordained ministry is that of the whole people of God. This, together with the conviction that all ministry derives from Christ and is always exercised through the power of the Spirit, forms the starting point. Within this shared conviction of the ecclesial, christological and pneumatological context, the texts move to the ministry, described variously as ordained, set apart or special. The transition is made through reference to the New Testament and the evidence of the early Church. The difficulty is that, where the evidence needs to be strongest to support a particular theology and order of ministry, it is in fact weakest. Such evidence is far from easy to handle in the concise form demanded of consensus texts and leads inevitably to questions being asked of it. For example, what are we to make of the likening of the emergence of a threefold order in the second half of the second century to the emergence of the Canon? Does this imply that such an order is binding on the Church in the same way as the Canon is binding? It appears from the Elucidation of the Ministry statement that the authors meant simply to underline the fact that both our Churches have retained that pattern. It is unlikely that we should infer that a threefold order is of the essence of the Church and therefore binding on a truly united Church of the future. The World Council statement, while not declaring a threefold order binding, does lean in the direction of its being desirable. 'The threefold ministry of bishop, presbyter and deacon may serve today as an expression of the unity we seek and also as a means of

55

achieving it.' Such a move in the direction of a threefold ministry challenges both our Churches which have retained the ancient pattern to search for more convincing ways of commending it to others, in the hope that it may indeed be an expression of unity and a means of achieving it.

When the various statements move on to describe the functions of ordained ministry, they focus on the specific responsibility for the proclamation of the word and the administration of the sacraments. The sharp division of the past between a Catholic sacramental priesthood and a Protestant ministry of the word has gone. The two are creatively held together, not in any attempt at unconvincing compromise but out of a genuine belief in their necessary interrelation.

A serious unresolved difference begins to appear in the various attempts to define the precise relationship between the ordained ministry and that of the whole people of God. In the World Council text this is placed in the commentary, showing that there is, as yet, no consensus in a multilateral context. It suggests that since the ordained ministry and the community are inextricably bound together, all members participate in fulfilling the same functions. But in defining what such shared functions are it appears to run into some difficulty and never quite makes clear whether the oversight of the community is shared by all, or is only a function of the ordained; neither is it clear how much, or how little, we are to infer from the statement that all may contribute to the sacramental life of the Body.

Most of the statements emphasize the representative nature of the ordained ministry. In Canterbury this is linked to the priestly vocation of the whole Church. It is however at this point that a difficulty arises. The priesthood of the ordained, while linked to the priesthood of the whole people of God, is called priestly—principally because it has a particular sacramental relationship to Christ as high priest. The president at the Eucharist 'is seen to stand in a sacramental relation to what Christ himself did in offering his own sacrifice'. In the Eucharist there is a sense in which the whole Body is united with Christ sacramentally in his self-offering and so shares his priesthood, but there is also (and the Elucidation enlarges on this) another sense in which the minister who presides, and only that minister, acts in a priestly way in the name of Christ on behalf of the Church, when he recites the narrative of institution and invokes the Spirit on the gifts. There are, according to the Elucidation, both the priesthood of all and the ministerial priesthood, which are distinct realities, each relating in its own way to the high priesthood of Christ. We are left in no doubt that the priesthood of the minister is not just a representative one of the whole Body, but is differentiated because of its relation to Christ's priesthood, focused in the eucharistic celebration. It is in this sense that we are to take the statement that ordained ministry 'is not an extension of the common Christian priesthood but belongs to another realm of the gifts of the Spirit'. Here is a genuine attempt to get behind the old divide between Protestants, who have talked of a difference of function and not of status, and Roman Catholics, who have maintained a difference in essence and not only of degree. We do seem to be groping together for a new understanding and a new language. But running throughout the ARCIC statements, as in other bilaterals, the explication of the relationships between ordained and lay is still problematic, carrying with it implications for the nature of the Church, for eucharistic practice, and for the exercise of authority in the Church. As Geoffrey Lampe once pointed out, 'The distinction between lay and clerical Christians is entirely absent from the Church of the New Testament period, and its introduction during the early centuries seems to have carried a confusion . . . from which it is extremely hard to extricate ourselves'.[4]

One of the most outstanding marks of convergence in the dialogues is in the understanding of apostolicity and apostolic succession. The context for understanding apostolicity in all the documents is seen as the whole tradition of the Church. The Church is apostolic in so far as it is faithful to the witness to Jesus Christ, given by the apostles, and in its communication of this witness to the world. The difficult area is in the precise relationship between succession in the broad sense, comprising the apostolic tradition of the Church as a whole and the apostolic succession of the ministry, and the particular sense which concerns the place of the episcopate as the indispensable sign of succession. Here the statement of the French 'Groupe des Dombes' has had considerable influence on many of the other discussions.[5] It talks of the bishop as the 'fullness of the sign', implying that Churches without episcopacy might still claim apostolic succession, while lacking the 'fullness of the sign'. The Lutheran-Roman Catholic statement is not so strong, with the 'valuable sign' and 'aspect of apostolicity', while Canterbury is much stronger and appears to say that the bishop is indeed an essential element. The World Council text, as a frame of reference, brings out that although there is not yet total agreement in a multilateral context on episcopacy as essential sign, yet we are in a much securer area for carrying the discussions further. The Churches which have episcopacy can now acknowledge a continuity in apostolic faith, worship and mission in those Churches which do not have the form of the historic episcopate, and Churches like our own are ready to acknowledge that, while episcopacy is indeed an 'essential' feature, it is not guarantee of the apostolicity of the Church. The importance of all this is obvious. The past situation of mutual disavowals is thankfully over. A way forward is opening up for a mutual recognition of ministries by episcopal and non-episcopal Churches in which neither side need deny its past but may rather look to a fuller expression of apostolicity in a united Church. Both Anglicans and Roman Catholics in bilateral conversations with non-episcopal Churches have reached similar conclusions. On this subject we can see clearly the effect the dialogues can have upon one another.

The discussion on the ordained ministry which led to the Canterbury text (1973) had as its subject matter the traditional male ministry as it had been received in both Churches. The rapid development within the Anglican Communion which led to a number of provinces ordaining women to the priesthood made it necessary by the time of the publication of *Elucidations* (1979) for the Commission to comment on the changed situation. From what they say, it would not appear that the Roman Catholic Church would be prevented from acknowledging the validity of the ministry of the Anglican Church simply by reason of the fact that women are ordained to the priesthood, but it is made clear that such ordinations present a grave obstacle to reconciliation.

What has been said in other dialogues involving the Roman Catholic Church forms an important context in which to view the work of ARCIC. The Reformed–Roman Catholic dialogue in the United States made a specific study of the role of women, including ordination of women to the priesthood. Its conclusion was: 'Because of the growing consensus among Reformed and Roman Catholic theologians that there is no insurmountable biblical or dogmatic obstacle to the ordination of women, and because of the needs of the people of God . . . we conclude that the ordination of women must be part of the church's life.'[6] More than this, it suggested that qualified women be admitted to ordination and that they be given 'full and equal participation in policy and decision making, and a voice in places of power, in the churches, at local, regional, national and world levels'.[7] More recently progress seems to have been made on this divisive issue in the Lutheran–Roman Catholic international conversations, where it is suggested that the ordination of women may not provide an insurmountable obstacle to the reconciliation of ministries. In the light of the official position of the Roman Catholic Church these are important statements for any who long to see both women priests and the reunion of the Anglican and Roman Catholic Churches and who are torn by what is so often presented to them as an either-or.

In the Anglican–Orthodox conversations there was no doubt about the effect such a move would have. The report of the joint Anglican–Orthodox Commission of 1978 contains a passionate plea from the Orthodox: 'In the name of our common Lord and Saviour Jesus Christ, we entreat our Anglican brothers not to proceed further with this action which is already dividing the Anglican Communion; and which will constitute a disastrous reverse for all our hopes of unity between Anglicanism and Orthodoxy.' The official Anglican response does not take up sides and is merely descriptive of the diversity of opinion on the matter within the Anglican Communion and the problems raised by it for the ways decisions are taken and where authority lies in such matters. What is clear from the strong language of this dialogue is how divisive an issue this remains.

The multilateral text of the World Council, with its insistence on the need to develop the role of women in the ministry of the Church, places its comments on ordination of women to the priesthood in commentary form, signifying this lack of agreement in the wide ecumenical scene. Anyone familiar with the heated discussions lying behind the carefully worded description will recognize the achievement which the final text represents. There are hopeful signs that, even on this most divisive of ecumenical problems, we are learning to listen to one another in the unique context of the World Council and to enter into a real exchange of views. 'Openness to each other holds out the possibility that the Spirit will speak to one Church through the insights of another', is an important sentence in the multilateral text.

The subject is an urgent one, as much within the Anglican Communion as between Anglicans and Roman Catholics and between Anglicans and Orthodox. Almost every meeting of an ecumenical group witnesses to the fact that it is a question that will not go away. It involves deep theological issues of creation, incarnation and ecclesiology which we must face together. A Church may be faced with the painful decision whether it should refuse to put into practice what it believes theologically to be true, for fear of slowing down the movement towards union. One of the first items on the agenda of the new ARCIC must be an investigation of the question of the ordination of women in the light of recent theological discussion and within the context of what has been said in other bilateral statements, particularly those in which one or other of our two Churches has been involved.

As with Eucharist, so with ministry, there is a remarkable convergence taking place. In the wider context of all the bilaterals the most welcome advance has been made in the area of the understanding of apostolicity and apostolic succession. However, there remain differences still on the place of the threefold order, the relationship between lay and ordained, the nature of priesthood and the problem of women's ordination. The ARCIC texts, not unexpectedly, show a much closer degree of agreement. Unfortunately we do not find here a statement on the theology of episcopacy that might have helped other bilateral dialogues in their task. Upholding as we do together the essential feature of episcopacy, the problem is how to deal with the fact of two parallel episcopates since the Reformation. The impasse of the disputed Anglican succession (*Apostolicae Curae* 1896) is not treated in the texts but is a question which must follow from such a close agreement on ministry as is surely found in the Canterbury text.

Of all the ARCIC material, that on Authority is the most exciting, but the area is the hardest to take hold of and leaves the most unresolved problems. The encapsulation of beliefs about authority in short statements makes for diffi- culty in comprehending what is being said and determining with any certainty the extent of the convergence reached. Nevertheless, the texts do repay detailed examination and it is impossible not to recognize in them a remarkable achievement. The concern is with authority in the Church and not with a comprehensive treatment of the authority of Scripture, tradition and traditions. Nevertheless there are many points in the texts where these subjects appear. Although the Commission cannot be held guilty, as they have been accused, of failing to give account of the primacy of Scripture, there lurk behind the texts basic questions about the authority and interpretation of Scripture, about the significance of the closing of the Canon, and about the dynamic or static nature of tradition, which will need to be taken up by ARCIC's successor. The questions are not unlike those raised in other dialogues, or in the important multilateral statement of the World Council published in 1963 on Scripture, Tradition and Traditions.[8]

In dealing with authority in the Church the argument progresses from the oversight of the ordained, through the bishop in the local church with his jurisdiction, to the coming together of bishops in councils at regional level , to the emergence of prominent sees with their jurisdiction, and eventually to the see of Rome with universal jurisdiction. At each stage the notions of primacy and conciliarity are harnessed together. It is important that the text moves, as it does, from the local church upwards. The Roman Church is so often caricatured as viewing the Church from the top down, a pyramid with sides sloping down from the Pope to bishops to priests to laity. The principle that nothing should be done in the Church at a higher level than is necessary – subsidiarity – means that central authority is viewed in quite another way. Rather than being the apex of the pyramid, it is that which gives service to the whole. Together with this welcome emphasis there is much else that is healing. At each stage in the unfolding of the picture, the exercise of oversight is linked to service for the building up of the fellowship of the Church. Time and time again there is the acknowledgement of past failure of the structures to reflect the authority of Christ. On the subject of the Bishop of Rome, there could hardly be a stronger statement of failures of the past. What emerges is a picture of an ideal structure and exercise of authority which contrasts markedly with its historic manifestation.

One of the questions Anglicans will ask is whether, in spite of this new shape, sufficient place is given to the role of the laity in the authoritative structures of the Church. Although the Elucidation of the first Authority statement attempts to answer this criticism by emphasizing a belief in the place of the laity in general, nothing is said more specifically about the laity in the exercise or criticism of authority. It is easy to make generalized statements about lay involvement and dispersed authority but to define the precise relation and interdependence of the lay and ordained functions remains a puzzle. Lay participation in the realm of authority is not simply confined to the participation of the few in conciliar bodies, for the mission, proclamation and safeguarding of the gospel 'involves the whole people of God', as the Commission declares. The *sensus fidelium* is necessary in the process of discernment and declaration of the truth of the gospel as it is transmitted and expressed from age to age. The Elucidation emphasizes that the *sensus fidelium* of the whole Church is vital in the reception of any decisions or statement. There is a welcome balance here which rejects the notion, on the one hand, that a conciliar definition has no authority apart from its acceptance by the whole Church, and, on the other, that a council is so self-sufficient that its 'definitions owe nothing to its acceptance'. In upholding both lay participation in synods and the part of the laity in witnessing to the *sensus fidelium*, the concept of authority moves away from a pattern of ministerial hierarchy built upon a paradigm of domination and subordination. To be committed to the different paradigm of authority implied throughout the Authority texts means discovering ways of drawing the whole community into the exercise of authority and of emphasizing both the right to criticize and the proper place for exercising discipline.

The argument moves step by step from the local church towards the claim for a universal primacy for the sake of unity. Universal primacy is seen as for service and as requiring the same complementarity on conciliarity needed at all levels of church life. The stress on collegial give and take could have a very important part to play in reshaping the functioning of the papacy, so that it may give effective service to other Churches which in any future union might expect a servant leader to respect their own pastoral needs. The potential of a universal primate as a sign of unity will be attractive to many Anglicans who recognize and indeed experience the value of signs and symbols, in particular the value of the personal as symbol. Although few would be able to explain it theologically, they do sense the importance of an archbishop or of the gathered bishops at the Lambeth Conference, as signs which transcend the particular and point beyond the local to an implied fellowship of Christians. ARCIC has been accused of arguing a case for universal primacy on historical rather than theological grounds, a distinction which in itself is hard to maintain rigidly. What is lacking in both the Ministry text, in relation to episcopacy, and in the Authority texts, is a theological argument for episcopacy which includes the necessity of the personal as sign of continuity and unity.

The real progress being made here on universal primacy has its closest parallel in the Lutheran–Roman Catholic dialogues. In the international dialogue there were hopeful signs of movement, and the Lutherans did not dismiss the office of papacy 'as a visible sign of the unity of the churches . . . in so far as it is subordinated to the primacy of the gospel by theological interpretation and practical restructuring'.[9] But the question whether the primacy of the Pope is necessary or just one possibility in the life of a Church remained unanswered. In the national dialogue in the United States the question of papal primacy was taken up again and makes a significant contribution to the discussion, showing how the statements of Vatican I on papacy with their anathemas can be viewed in a new light, and how the leadership of the Bishop of Rome might incorporate more fully the three principles which surfaced at Vatican II, legitimate diversity, collegiality and subsidiarity. At the end of the dialogue, the prospects of a renewed papacy were, as one of the Roman Catholic participants described, so exciting to the Lutheran theologians that they joined with their Roman Catholic partners in asking the Lutheran Churches:

If they are prepared to affirm with us that Papal Primacy, renewed in the light of the Gospel, need not be a barrier to reconciliation.

If they are able to acknowledge . . . the possibility and desirability of the Papal Ministry, renewed under the Gospel and committed to Christian freedom, in a large communion which would include Lutheran Churches.

Such convergence in both the Anglican and Lutheran dialogues with the Roman Catholic Church is not yet matched in the work of the multilateral World Council text where there is no move in the direction of a universal primacy. However, at the final session at which the texts were declared mature enough to be referred to the Churches the question of the Petrine office was raised for the first time and serious thought was given to whether or not some statement might be included in commentary form. It was deemed too late to include this, but the intention was expressed of taking up the investigation in future work of the Faith and Order Commission. This may well reflect the significant moves in this direction in the bilateral dialogues, and bear witness to the way in which convergence in one dialogue has wider implications.

This move in the texts in the direction of a universal primacy, serving the fellowship of the Church, in conciliarity, providing a strong cohesive force and at the same time respecting and allowing a proper diversity, is a

significant move in the history of the ecumenical movement. The objection, however, that Anglicans and many
others would raise, would be to the particular claims that
have developed in history in relation to the Roman primacy,
and it is to that that the Commission bravely turned in
Authority II.

The old claim that papacy in its developed form can be
read back into the New Testament is shown to be no longer
tenable and what is said about the Petrine texts is very
restrained indeed. What is important is the reassertion of
the place of a universal primacy in a reunited Church. Such
a primacy would appropriately be modelled on the role of
Peter and attached to the see of Rome.

The second Authority statement makes no use of the
idea of a Petrine tradition traceable within the New
Testament, which establishes a Petrine trajectory beginning
during Peter's own life-time and continuing after his death,
an idea which plays a prominent part in the Lutheran-
Roman Catholic dialogue. In that dialogue the claims for
the Petrine office made in Vatican I are judged, not simply
on whether they are verifiable in the career of the historical
Simon, but also on whether they are consonant with the
trajectory of images of Peter in the New Testament and
beyond. The question in that dialogue has become, to what
extent has the trajectory of Peter's images culminated in
the papacy as it exists today? This is a suggestive use of the
biblical material which does justice to the dynamic quality
of biblical traditions and does not involve the same break
with the New Testament material as underlies the ARCIC
text.

The new text on Authority concludes with a treatment of
the most difficult of all issues, the question of what kind of
teaching authority belongs to the Bishop of Rome. The
term infallibility, which carries with it so many unhelpful
connotations from the past, is avoided as far as possible and
the question is clearly put: is there 'a special ministerial gift
of discerning the truth of teaching, bestowed at crucial

times on one person to enable him to speak authoritatively in the name of the Church in order to preserve the people of God in truth'? As the text unfolds we find many welcome emphases upon the teaching authority of councils and a universal primate working together, and reception by the people of God as the ultimate vindication that a matter of faith has been preserved from error. It is agreed that definitions of matters of faith are always made in the 'terms of the understanding and framework of their age' and when they safeguard the 'substance of faith' then they have a lasting significance. But after all this we arrive at the description of two differing positions: that of Roman Catholics who argue that, if certain conditions are fulfilled, a judgement is preserved from error, and that of Anglicans who, if a statement were not manifestly in line with biblical faith and orthodox tradition, would want to put it to the test of study and discussion. In the context it is very hard to pinpoint and to explicate the precise area of disagreement, and this surely needs further working out.

In the course of the statement consideration is given to the two Marian dogmas, showing the measure of agreement on Mary as a 'model of holiness, obedience and faith for all Christians'. Even if these lines point to a rediscovery of Mary which is neither a foreign imposition on Anglican thought nor a denial of past Roman Catholic thought and piety, the interpretation of the Marian dogmas is not ultimately the question but rather the process by which such statements were made and whether they are fixed for all time and would be binding on any united Church of the future.

The convergence without consensus reflected in ARCIC has a close parallel in the lengthier and rather more exciting text of the Lutheran–Roman Catholic dialogue which shows a reassessment of popular assumptions and theological interpretations on the part of the Roman Catholic members and a real move to see papal teaching authority in a more favourable light by the Lutherans.[10] The context in which infallibility is set is not dissimilar from that of the Venice text, with emphasis upon the authority of the gospel and its relation to Scripture and tradition and the structures of the Church, a relinquishing of the old divide between *sola scriptura* on the one hand and the teaching magisterium of the Church on the other, and a shared agreement on the indefectibility of the Church and belief that absolute infallibility belongs to God alone and limited and conditional infallibility to the Pope.

Here, as in ARCIC, differences of emphasis are acknowledged, but it is similarly difficult to be sure, as the Lutheran participants themselves confess, what disagreement between the two sides in fact amounts to. Clearly we are in a new position, for what these two dialogues state about infallibility is not that which has been so often feared in the past and which has been the subject of such bitter attack. It has to be acknowledged that some differences of emphasis remain and we ought not to minimize the gulf that separates popular thought from the position of these two statements. But a bridge has been built and both dialogues show that positions are not polarized. As ARCIC itself says, 'Contemporary discussions of conciliarity and primacy in both communions indicate that we are not dealing with positions destined to remain static'. The question will have to be asked whether, even if Anglicans cannot accept the particular nature of the teaching authority of the Bishop of Rome for themselves, it has to be a barrier to the unity of our Churches.

One of the most welcome things to emerge from the work of ARCIC taken as a whole is a picture, incomplete though it is, of what unity and diversity might mean in a united Church. There is an emphasis both on the need for unity to be focused in structures and persons transcending the local, and also on the need for a proper diversity which is never stifled. A Church that has a universal primate, not divorced from collegiality, a servant figure focusing unity, should be able to tolerate and sustain more, not less, diversity than other churches. Those who are conscious of the brokenness of the Church will be drawn to the benefits and potentialities of such an effectual sign. Underlying this picture of unity and diversity is the concept of *koinonia* (communion). It is this which holds the three statements together, as Eucharist is understood as the effectual sign of community, *episcope* its servant and primacy its focus. *Koinonia* as both the goal and the way is far less limiting or static a concept than either organic union or conciliar fellowship. The riches and depths of *koinonia* will only be unfolded as the journey progresses with greater openness and commitment to one another.

The range of opinion in the Anglican Church and the existence of conservative elements in both our Churches mean that there will be no unqualified or unreserved acceptance of the statements. Anglican and Roman Catholic theologians will continue to discuss them and contribute to a necessary and informed debate. There are unresolved differences witnessed to in the texts – on the ordination of women and the teaching authority of the Bishop of Rome; there are puzzles contained in the Commission's own convergence – on the relation of ordained to lay ministry; and there are emerging related problems underlying the Commission's treatment of authority – Scripture and tradition, the significance of the closing of the Canon, and the need to articulate a fuller theology of episcopacy. Nevertheless it would be difficult for even those who are most wedded to sixteenth-century formularies not to welcome the change in climate in which these discussions took place, the humble acknowledgement of past failures, and the genuine attempt to get behind entrenched positions of the past in order to chart new paths for the future. The texts represent much more than the results of a group of likeminded, similarly trained theologians who in the process of working together have acquired a common outlook no longer related to the positions of their own

Churches. They are the most important of all ecumenical texts of this century and are signs of hope not only for the Churches involved but for the whole ecumenical movement.

The statements challenge us to act. To receive them and remain where we are would be to fail to recognize the signs of hope in them. The members of the Commission testify to the importance of their shared explorations. The experience of engaging together in discussion enabled them to enter into one another's thoughts and to move towards a common understanding. If the convergence they represent is not to remain the preserve of a theological élite, shared discussion of the texts needs to take place as widely as possible. The ARCIC texts, more than any other bilateral texts, have been discussed by national commissions. Now there is need to widen the base of discussion by using the texts in theological colleges and in lay education to enable as many as possible to take part in the process of growing into union.

If what is said in the texts is not contrary to the beliefs of our Churches, and, if we can recognize in them our faith, then discussion, on however wide a basis, is not enough. The texts challenge us to ask whether there is not sufficient agreement to extend eucharistic hospitality. It is in the Eucharist that many Anglicans and Roman Catholics feel the pain of separation most, at the local level where churches often work closely together, as well as at national or international gatherings. Furthermore, the agreement reflected in the ministry text must challenge the Roman Catholic Church to reconsider its position with regard to Anglican Orders. Is it time now to recognize one another's ministries and become reconciled as a further stage on the way towards the realization of *koinonia*?

Moreover, the texts and the decisions stimulated by them surely form a basis for further theological dialogues as a necessary continuation of the journey. If it is true that experience influences the perception and understanding of truth, then the community which interprets for us must be as representative as possible. ARCIC contained neither representatives from the Third World nor women members, and this is unfortunately reflected in the style and language of the statements. This is in marked contrast to the World Council Statements, where the language embraces a worldwide community both in its constant reference to the goal 'that the world might believe' and in the nature of its illustrative examples; they avoid any language that could be accused of excluding women. It is hard to make this point without appearing trivial, but if the unity of the Church has to do with a community that does not exclude, this must be mirrored in the language of theological statement. A new Commission must include amongst its members women and representatives of a worldwide Church.

Finally the work of ARCIC presents a challenge to recognize the movement of our two Churches as part of a much wider movement towards unity. Although there are problems in comparing the bilateral and multilateral dialogues because of their different starting points, aims and agendas, nevertheless it is possible to detect significant and hopeful convergences in many areas which would have been unthinkable only a few years ago. In this wider movement Catholic and Protestant traditions contribute towards an emerging Christian tradition. This has happened partly through the interaction and influence of one dialogue upon another. This must be encouraged to continue so that there will never be such a thing as a 'pure bilateral'. Advance in one dialogue must strengthen the resolve to work with other partners with whom we are at quite different stages of convergence. There can be no room for rival ecumenisms within the one movement towards unity. Advance on one front must never be seen as erecting barriers on another. To rejoice over the achievements of ARCIC must strengthen and not weaken commitment to the wider ecumenical movement.

The movement towards unity is not a race to be won by

any two parties but a pilgrimage to be lived. On the way we prepare ourselves to receive, in God's own time and not in our own, the goal. It is a pilgrimage which involves risks and the pain of surrendering what is often, if only we would recognize it, already over and outlived, for the sake of better and richer things. There is a real sense in which the ecumenical journey means dying in order to receive fuller life – the *koinonia* of the unbroken Body of Christ.

NOTES

1 *The Three Agreed Statements*: Eucharistic Doctrine, Ministry and Ordination, Authority in the Church (SPCK and CTS 1978) have been followed by a second statement on Authority and published with supporting material as *The Final Report* (SPCK and CTS 1982).

2 *One Baptism, One Eucharist and a Mutually Recognised Ministry*, Faith and Order Paper 73, 1975.

3 *Elucidations* (SPCK and CTS 1979) is now incorporated in *The Final Report*, which also includes an Elucidation of the first Authority statement.

4 G. W. H. Lampe, *Explorations in Theology* (1981), p. 93.

5 Group of Les Dombes, *Towards a Reconciliation of Ministries*, 1973.

6 *Ministry in the Church* (1971), No. 4.

7 *Women in the Church*, p. 239.

8 *Scripture, Tradition and Traditions*, The Fourth World Conference on Faith and Order, Montreal 1963.

9 *Papal Primacy and the Universal Church*, Lutherans and Catholics in Dialogue V.

10 *Teaching Authority and Infallibility in the Church*, Lutheran–Roman Catholic Dialogue 1978.

4

'Artisans of a New Humanity'?

Some Anglican and Roman Catholic approaches to social and political action

Kenneth Leech

I want in this chapter to examine some aspects of the social and political involvement of Anglicans and Roman Catholics in England in recent years. If we are to make sense of this, some theological and historical perspective is necessary. The 'social tradition' of the Church of England has been the subject of considerable research and documentation. F. D. Maurice is rightly seen as the key theological influence. While Maurice's political standpoint was extremely conservative and his direct involvement in social action negligible, his theological perspective shaped several generations of social activists in the Church. It was the fusion of Maurician theology with the ritualism of the late Tractarian 'slum priests' in the East End of London and elsewhere which led to the vigorous social radicalism of such groups as the Guild of St Matthew, the Catholic Crusade and the more cautious but very influential groups such as the Christian Social Union, the League of the Kingdom of God, the Christendom Group, and so on. Such figures as B. F. Westcott, Henry Scott Holland, Charles Gore and William Temple were products of this tradition of social theology with its strong incarnational and sacramental emphasis. Its practical manifestations can be seen in the social utterances of successive Lambeth Conferences (especially those of 1888, 1896 and 1920), in the active involvement of Anglicans in the inner city problems of the late Victorian era and beyond, and in the movement of thought which culminated in Temple's work and the Oxford Conference on Church, Community and State of 1937.[1]

The history of social thought in the Roman Catholic community was quite different. The theoretical basis for a concern for social justice was contained in a series of 'social encyclicals' from Leo XIII's *Rerum Novarum* of 1891 onwards. In Britain the teaching of the social encyclicals was propagated by the very respectable Catholic Social Guild. The early encyclicals were marked by a strong anti-communist flavour which tended to dominate them, obscuring the wider concern for justice and for a just economic order. *Divini Redemptoris* of Pius XI (1937), the first encyclical to name Marx (though only in passing), was concerned with the Bolshevist threat to Christian order and saw Communism as a mortal sickness, intrinsically evil, a movement with which no collaboration was possible. *Quadragesimo Anno* (1931) condemned even 'mitigated Social-ism'. It simply was not possible to be a Catholic and a Socialist. These were the years when committed groups of Socialists were influencing many Anglicans. However the social encyclicals were also strongly critical of capitalism and of the concentration of wealth and power, of the excesses of competition, and the 'international imperialism of money' (QA para. 109).

The entire emphasis and perspective of the encyclicals of John XXIII and Paul VI was markedly different. *Mater et Magistra* (1961) and *Pacem in Terris* (1963) of John XXIII are landmarks. The analysis of Socialist and Marxist thought by Pope Paul VI in *Populorum Progressio* (1967) and *Octogesima Adveniens* (1971) is careful and thoughtful. These encyclicals both reflected, and helped to shape, the changing consciousness of Roman Catholic social thought. Since then, the encyclicals of Pope John Paul II, in particular *Redemptor Hominis* (1980) and *Laborem Exercens* (1981), have emphasized human dignity and the demands of social justice.

So, while in the Roman Catholic community, we see a series of authoritative, magisterial documents relating to social thought, the pattern in the Church of England is rather of the influence of a number of individual thinkers which comes later to be reflected in the statements of conferences and commissions. This difference is, of course, one which runs throughout the history of the two communions, and indicates the differing understandings of authority and of theological method.

In recent years, the most significant feature of the official documents from the various Churches has been the clear evidence of a convergence of positions on social justice and the theological basis of Christian social action. The documents of the Second Vatican Council, in particular *Gaudium et Spes*, are of fundamental importance in understanding the shift which has occurred. We have seen a richer doctrine of grace with a rejection of earlier 'two planes' spirituality and a strong emphasis on the integrity of the human person. The stress on man, on the need to work for a new world and to oppose sin in its social and structural forms comes through even more strongly in the document *Justice in the World* of 30 November 1971, the statement of the Third Synod of Bishops. This Synod represented 'a turning point for Catholic social teaching', and it has been argued that in the formal statements of this period we have seen 'a decided shift to the left in the official teaching documents of the Christian churches'.[2] For it was in this period also that we saw the growing concern with development (which entered the theological vocabulary after Bandung (1955)) and with liberation in the thought of the World Council of Churches. The World Conference on Church and Society at Geneva in July 1966 was a major landmark in ecumenical social thought. It seems clear that, on the main theological approach to social justice, the Roman Catholic Church and the Churches represented in the World Council of Churches now show a remarkable similarity on all essential matters, and it has been claimed that this is also increasingly true of the method by which documents are produced.[3]

However the positions taken in formal documents do not necessarily reflect a corresponding change in outlook in the respective Churches nationally or locally. Does the average Roman Catholic read encyclicals, or the average Anglican know anything of the Lambeth Conferences or of the tradition of social thought in the Church? A recent survey of Roman Catholic opinion in England and Wales showed that only half of those interviewed had ever heard of the Second Vatican Council and that two-thirds of younger Catholics had not heard of it. There was 'little awareness of any ideological implications in the conciliar teaching'.[4] At a recent meeting of Roman Catholic bishops, only three were familiar with the 1971 Synod document. Only one head-teacher of a Roman Catholic school in one area had ever heard of it. Similarly, more Anglicans would share the view of Christianity reflected in the pages of the *Daily Telegraph* than that stated in the theological traditions of their own Church.

This does not, of course, mean that official or semi-official teaching documents are of no importance. They are important in at least two ways. First they do, on a long-term basis, change the direction and the atmosphere of thought and action in the Church. Secondly, they provide essential ammunition and resource material for those engaged in struggles who can often draw on the teaching documents of the Church as a way of defending their orthodoxy. (Witness the experience of liberation theologies in South America.) Yet the popular image of the Church's witness may be shaped more by the events of the past – the missed opportunity of the General Strike, the anti-union speeches of certain prelates, the deeply held feeling that Anglicans are Tories and that, while Roman Catholics tend to vote Labour, the Church Establishment is not on the side of

working people. These impressions survive long after their
validity has been eroded by developments. Again, neither
Church in England has been marked in recent years by any
serious attempt to evolve a theology of social justice. There
has been considerable practical and theoretical work on
specific issues (industrial affairs, moral decisions, etc.) by
Boards for Social Responsibility and by the various
commissions. But much of the theology remains woolly
and unclear, and there is considerable work to be
done.

I want now to examine three areas in which there has
been considerable practical collaboration between Roman
Catholics, Anglicans and others, and to show how quite
different patterns appear in the form this has taken.

First, the area of *peace and war*. For many years the
hierarchies of both Churches have issued strong general
condemnations of modern warfare, but there was a sense of
the incongruity between what the Church said and what it
did. The creation of Pax, a Roman Catholic peace movement,
in September, 1936, was an early example of ecumenical co-
operation and of the way in which Roman Catholics and
Anglicans who were committed to working for peace
worked together in isolation from their Churches and were
often severely criticized by them. Pax used the teachings of
Scripture, the Fathers, St Thomas Aquinas and the papal
encyclicals to defend its opposition to war. It supported the
right of conscientious objection and attacked the attitudes
to war in the more 'official' Catholic publications. There
was a joint Conference of Pax and the Anglican Pacifist
Fellowship on 24 June 1940 at St Anne's, Soho, where,
thirty years later, another important ecumenical initiative
in the care of the homeless was to occur (see below). *Pax
Bulletin* in 1950 publicized the Pastoral Letter of the French
Cardinals and Archbishops and Cardinal Ottaviani's clear
statement that a just war was impossible in modern
conditions.

In the 1950s the debate on nuclear weapons produced

varied reactions from Roman Catholic and Anglican leaders. Both Cardinal Griffin and Archbishop Garbett condemned the hydrogen bomb but said that Britain should manufacture it. The 'better dead than red' thesis was used by several leading Anglican bishops, though Michael Ramsey as Archbishop of York described it as 'appalling' that such a thesis should come from any Christian lips. Between 1954 and 1958 (when the Campaign for Nuclear Disarmament began) there were condemnations of H-bomb tests (as by the Pope on Palm Sunday 1957 and the *Catholic Herald* on 15 June 1956). Lord Cherwell, in the House of Lords on 8 May 1957, strongly deplored the Pope's words. Even unilateral nuclear disarmament received support from some Anglican bishops (such as William Greer of Manchester and Glyn Simon of Llandaff) while both the Campaign for Nuclear Disarmament and the Committee of 100 contained members of both Churches among their leaders. Of the first group to be imprisoned for anti-bomb activities in 1958, two were Anglican communicants. At the same period, Archbishop Thomas Roberts SJ, former Archbishop of Bombay, was openly supporting the cause of nuclear disarmament and the Committee of 100. In 1960 he was 'delated' to Rome by the Apostolic Delegate on various charges, including associating with Pax and taking part in conferences of Christian Action. In 1961 Cardinal Godfrey forbade him to read prayers on Remembrance Sunday in Trafalgar Square at a meeting of CND. However, while these isolated figures were important prophetic voices, it cannot be said that the Christian community as such played a major role in the anti-bomb movement of the early 1960s. Only much later, when the cause became respectable, did it attract increasing support from churches and church leaders.

In 1968, Monsignor Bruce Kent told the Annual Meeting of Pax, that 'the Peace Movement in Catholic circles looks as if it is about to become respectable'. The Second Vatican Council had only stopped short, under pressure from some

American bishops, of condemnation of the possession of nuclear weapons. Since then we have seen a growing rejection of the policies of nuclear deterrence among the leadership of the Churches. The discussions initiated by CADD (Christian Approaches to Defence and Disarmament), originally founded as an alternative to unilateralism, have played a significant role in this shift. In 1979 the Assembly of the British Council of Churches opposed the renewal of the independent deterrent, and it seems likely that similar positions will appear from discussions which are taking place among Anglicans. As yet there is no English parallel to the forthright condemnation of nuclear deterrence in the 1976 statement of the American Roman Catholic Bishops' Conference, *To Live in Christ Jesus*, or in the call by Archbishop Raymond Hunthausen of Seattle to Christians to withhold part of their taxes as a protest against nuclear weapons.[5]

It would be wrong to end this section on peace and war without reference to the vitally important ecumenical role played since 1940 by the Sword of the Spirit, which in 1965 became the Catholic Institute for International Relations. Under the inspired leadership of Mildred Neville, the CIIR has provided a major resource point for the creation and nourishing of an informed Christian conscience on world affairs and matters of peace and justice.[6]

Secondly, the area of *homelessness*. There had been some localized campaigning around the issue of the urban homeless in the 1950s. The hostels of the Salvation Army, Church Army, and such Roman Catholic communities as the Providence Row refuge had for many years housed many homeless persons. But it was the creation of the Simon Community and its 'mission to the misfit' in 1963 which led to a series of events, culminating in the expansion of concern for the 'homeless and rootless' into a national campaign. Anton Wallich-Clifford, a devout Roman Catholic and a Franciscan tertiary, found, as a probation officer at Bow Street, that increasing numbers of his clients were classified 'N.F.A.' (No Fixed Abode). Anton was deeply influenced by the work of Dorothy Day, Peter Maurin and the Catholic Worker 'houses of hospitality' in the poor districts of American cities, and the early Simon houses were modelled on those of the Catholic Worker. Anton's vision of a new-style religious order of drop-outs, under the patronage of Simon of Cyrene, never materialized. Most Simon workers did not share its founder's Christian faith, and his concern to 'see Christ in every shattered body'. His movement has been described by one critical writer on homelessness as a Victorian romantic movement with a touch of Gothic. But it was the Simon Community, more than any other group, which rejected the labelling and classifying of the homeless, and insisted on a simple equality.

Out of Simon grew the Cyrenians, while other pioneering movements grew up named after St Mungo, St Dismas, and others. In November 1969, as a result of considerable co-operation over some years between Anton and the present writer, Centrepoint was established at St Anne's House in Soho. This was the first all-night crisis centre for the young homeless in London, offering emergency accommodation and staffed by eight volunteers each night, without whose help the project would never have survived. Many of these were Roman Catholic seminarians and Religious. There was particular collaboration with the Servite Order who had established Benburb Base in London as a centre for homeless Irish youth. So here, where once Pax and St Anne's Society had met, a new phase of Anglican–Roman Catholic co-operation began which also marked a new stage in Simon's work, a move from care of the derelict to preventive work. Closely linked with Centrepoint was the Christian Action Shelter for homeless women in nearby Greek Street; and later Centrepoint joined with other West End projects to form a federation of campaigning groups. Parallel with this cluster of projects, and closely linked with them, was the pioneering work of Fr Eamonn Casey (now

Bishop of Galway) in the Shelter Housing Action Centre
(SHAC) which grew from the Catholic Housing Aid Society
(CHAS). It was as a result of this early work with the
London homeless that the Campaign for the Homeless and
Rootless (CHAR) was established. The full story of the
involvement of Roman Catholics and Anglicans in helping
to lay the foundations of this major movement of social
action has still to be written.

Alongside this work of providing crisis help for the
homeless there was a growing pressure on the hierarchies of
the two Churches to take up positions on housing and
homelessness. The Anglican bishops of London and South-
wark had led a march to draw attention to the needs of the
homeless in the early 1960s while Crisis at Christmas,
formed at the end of the 60s, received support from the
Archbishop of Canterbury among other church leaders.
The former Bishop of London, Gerald Ellison, addressed
himself, in the House of Lords and in letters to the press, to
the concerns expressed by CHAR. However, the joint
statement by Bishop Ellison and Cardinal Hume, in May
1981, marked a turning point in official responses and was
probably the first example of a public statement by bishops
which moved beyond general concern to support for
specific changes in the law, in this case the Housing Bill.

In the field of homelessness, we have seen a shift from
small-scale rescue work to pressure group activity at a
centrally organized level, with both Anglicans and Roman
Catholics playing important roles along with non-Christians
at each level.

Thirdly, the area of *racial justice*. Again, there had been
localized work, especially in London, Manchester, Birming-
ham and other cities, among Commonwealth immigrants
from the late 1940s onwards. The work of the Anglican
Franciscans in Stepney from 1944 onwards, of Bernard Ball
in Moss Side in the 1950s, or of the Congregationalist
Clifford Hill in Tottenham in the early 1960s, are among
many examples. But there was little organized Christian

resistance to racism even though the anti-black campaigners were gathering strength in the 50s and played an important role in the 1958 riots in Notting Hill. There was virtually no opposition from the Church at national level to the clearly racist provisions of the 1962 Commonwealth Immigrants Act, apart from a speech by Archbishop Ramsey in the Lords describing the measure as 'lamentable'. Most church leaders apparently saw no problem which a measure of good neighbourliness could not solve. It is striking to notice how little was said about the growing multi-ethnic composition of British society in otherwise well-informed reports from church bodies. Thus, the Durham Report, *The Fourth R*, on religious education, published in 1970, virtually ignored the question apart from a passing reference.

However, in 1965 the CIIR set up a Race Relations Advisory Group, and six months later approached Cardinal Heenan to suggest the appointment of a social worker. In February 1968 Lewis Donnelly was appointed as adviser to the hierarchy on race, and out of his early work grew the Catholic Commission for Racial Justice, the most effective and dynamic of the four commissions.

Meanwhile, the Community and Race Relations Unit (CRRU) had been set up in 1971 at the British Council of Churches, and soon established a reputation as a resource centre for the churches and others. An invaluable element within CRRU has been its Projects Fund, which has given considerable financial help to hundreds of projects throughout Britain. After considerable debate, the General Synod of the Church of England committed itself to support the Fund and commended it to the dioceses, and in 1981 a Race Relations Field Officer was appointed to the staff of the Board for Social Responsibility (BSR).

The collaboration between CCRJ, CRRU and BSR has been very close and effective, and was particularly evident in the well-organized and well-informed campaign against the British Nationality Bill of 1981. This began with a

statement by the Roman Catholic bishops which was then
approved by the BCC and by the House of Bishops of the
Church of England. There were also regular bulletins and
briefings of both hierarchies, a filmstrip which was shown
throughout the country, and close collaboration with
bodies such as the Joint Council for the Welfare of
Immigrants (JCWI) and the Action Group on Immigration
and Nationality (AGIN). So great was the opposition that
the Government seemed to find it difficult to understand
that the Churches had not been 'got at' by sinister political
forces: it did not seem to have occurred to some ministers,
for example, that church leaders might actually have
studied the question and reached a conclusion on the basis
of the evidence! Considerable pressure was brought on
bishops, both by letter and, on at least one occasion, by a
personal visit from a minister, to moderate their opposition
in the interests of 'national stability'.

However, the increasingly vocal opposition to institutional racism by a number of bishops, and the effectiveness
of the well-informed anti-racist groups within the churches,
should not obscure the fact that the consciousness of racial
disadvantage and racial oppression is not always evident in
the churches nationally and locally. Both Churches remain
overwhelmingly white Churches within a multi-racial
society. Neither CRRU nor CCRJ has managed to get
across to the majority of parishes. Even parishes in multi-
racial areas have difficulty in recognizing the issues. Thus
race was one of five 'priorities' chosen at the Area Pastoral
Assembly in East London on 21 October 1979. But at the
Assembly on 22 February 1981 it was reported that 'very
little – even nothing – had been done under this priority.
Some found it difficult to identify the problem and so there
was little perception that anything needed to be done.'[7]

Finally, what are the opportunities and the difficulties in
future co-operation and in the development of work for
social justice in the two Churches? A number of areas stand
out which demand careful attention.

First, the *insularity* of English Christianity from the world Church and world issues. The lack of awareness not only of theological thinking but also of social and political involvement in the churches of Africa, Asia and North and South America is serious enough. But there is also a continuing isolation of English churchpeople, heavily concentrated in the suburbs, from the actual live options for most nations. So questions which are daily bread and butter matters for Christians in many parts of the world are often seen as subjects for committee discussion in English church circles. It is possible too that there is a similar isolation of English Roman Catholics from the atmosphere of the international Catholic community. The insularity of English church life is therefore a serious obstacle to a dialogue which takes account of the worldwide movements of Christian thought and action.

Secondly, the question of *class*. The numerical strength of the Church of England lies in the suburban dioceses, and its weakness in the inner-city working class districts is well known and well documented. It has never, as a Church, had a 'feel' for the culture of the urban working class, or for the Labour movement. The Roman Catholic Church in England presents a striking contrast with a high percentage to be found in the semi-skilled and unskilled manual occupations, and low ratios among managerial and professional groups. No other religious group has a greater percentage in the lowest class group or a lower percentage among non-manual workers. Yet, because of its fear of socialism and its character as a mainly migrant church, the alienation from working-class life has been encouraged. Both Churches need to devote much thought, prayer and energy to the overcoming of the class barrier which cuts them off in many areas from the mass of the people.

Thirdly, the attitude to *politics*. There is a deep fear of political conflict in both Churches, and a persisting sense that the purpose of religion is to comfort rather than to transform. In spite of the important work of the Industrial Christian Fellowship in the past, and of the Young Christian Workers within the Roman Catholic community, the fear of political action is very deep-rooted in both Churches. 'Otherworldliness' was described by a leading Roman Catholic bishop in 1950 as the dominant character-istic of the Catholic.[8] The tendency of Catholics to vote Labour does not seem to be based on any particular awareness of a political dynamic deriving from gospel values: indeed, that tendency seems to decline as parish activity increases![9]

'Catholics do appear to display a commitment to social justice, at least in principle, but they are rather more hesitant about the means required for its promotion. They are relatively divided on the particular obligations which a desire for social justice lays upon them, and in particular they are unwilling to regard such obligations as extending towards political involvement.'[10] That would be equally applicable to Anglicans. On the other hand we have seen in recent years an increased willingness for church leaders to take up political issues, and a corresponding willingness for government spokesmen to criticize them for doing so, emphasizing the 'spiritual' role of the Church.[11]

Fourthly, the 'Irish-ness' of the Roman Catholic Church in England. For the early Irish immigrants the Church was a support and an identity, and this led to the emergence of inward-looking, defensive, tightly-knit parishes.[12] The migrant character of the community discouraged any active interest in social and political concerns which were per-ceived as English. The Irish parochial culture has not helped in the integration of the black community who find themselves celebrating St Patrick (without having much idea who he was) and are faced with parish parties where the ceilidh band is a necessary element. On the other hand, the inflexibility of successive English governments over Northern Ireland and the apparent inability of most English people to comprehend the issues involved have not encouraged any real ecumenical progress at a grass-roots level.

Fifthly, the question of *clericalism*. Traditionally, the Roman Catholic priest has played a dominant role in liturgical and doctrinal matters, though lay involvement in the parochial administration and in other fields has often exceeded that of Anglican parishes. Evangelical Anglicans have for long stressed the role of the laity in evangelism and in Christian ministry, while Anglo-Catholics have had great difficulty in escaping from their clerical captivity.

However, there is a serious problem that in relation to social and political attitudes, the gulf between clergy and laity in both Churches may be widening. An American sociologist, writing over ten years ago, referred to this as a 'widening gap'[13] and saw it as a source of trouble for the future. In many Anglican parishes, the relatively liberal/ *Guardian* views of the clergy may be in sharp contrast with the attitudes of their conservative/*Telegraph*-reading congregations. In the Roman Catholic Church there may also be a gulf between the politically committed priests (a minority, mainly Religious, and strongly influenced by radical movements in the Third World) and the secular clergy. Certainly, political involvement of clergy has been frowned upon. The 1971 Synod, which issued the influential document on justice, also produced *The Ministerial Priesthood* which urged priests to maintain a 'certain distance' from political parties except in 'concrete and exceptional circumstances'.

Sixthly, the question of access to accurate *data*. One of the most important aspects of the work of the CIIR and CCRJ has been their effectiveness in supplying the hierarchy with accurate and thoroughly researched information. A similar role has been played by the Board for Social Responsibility of the Church of England, by CRRU, by the various pressure groups in the fields mentioned above. There is no doubt that this improvement in briefing procedures has contributed to an increase in the quality of episcopal pronouncements. The public contributions of both Anglican and Roman Catholic bishops on housing, urban conflict and issues of war and peace have shown that such briefings have had their effect.

At the same time, there is still room for improvement at the less formal level. Public utterances must be rooted in factual accuracy. Bishops are still prone to make comments in sermons which reflect their own cultural milieu more than their grasp of reality. Thus the present Archbishop of Canterbury, in his 1980 Christmas Sermon, chose to attack high-rise flats, though there has been virtually no high-rise building since 1968. One well-respected bishop with an excellent social record stated, in a discussion about the joint initiative on homelessness by Cardinal Hume and Bishop Ellison, that 'the significance of the Bishop of London and Cardinal Hume signing something together was worthwhile, *even if they got it wrong*' (my italics).

Finally, and perhaps more important, the *character*, *status* and *clientèle* of the two Churches is changing. The Church of England still sees itself as a national Church though it is the only branch of the Anglican Communion in which the bulk of the membership is lapsed. 'Many church leaders in England still think of themselves as influential national figures (as they are in law) rather than as leaders of a relatively small Christian community in a largely secular State (as they are in fact).'[14] Indeed, one of the deep worries which lies behind the current debate over liturgical reform is about the status of the Church vis-à-vis the nation: is the Church now ceasing to be a Church for all people, including those with no clear Christian belief, and becoming a more doctrinaire denominational grouping with clearer boundaries and a minority character? If it is, is it desirable or not?

Until recently, the Roman Catholic hierarchy, with the spectacular exception of Cardinal Manning, has tended not to take an active role in national political issues. However, there is evidence that both the hierarchy and the Church as a whole, which has traditionally been a minority church, concerned with the spiritual care of its members rather than with a responsibility for its neighbourhood and the community outside the church, may now be changing and moving towards a more outward-looking stance.

Perhaps the really decisive question facing the two Churches in the next decade is: Will they accept the role of 'established Churches', ministering to and speaking for a residually Christian nation? Or will they seek to be prophetic minorities, diminished in size but stronger in integrity, a creative remnant, disturbing leaven, ready to be, in the words of the Second Vatican Council, 'the artisans of a new humanity'?

NOTES

1 See John Oliver, *The Church and Social Order: Social Thought in the Church of England 1918-1939* (Mowbrays 1968).

2 Gregory Baum, *The Social Imperative* (New York, Paulist Press 1979), pp. 75, 174.

3 Ronald H. Preston, *Explorations in Theology 9* (SCM 1981), p. 28.

4 Michael P. Hornsby-Smith and Raymond M. Lee, *Roman Catholic Opinion. A Study of Roman Catholics in England and Wales in the 1970s. Final Report* (Dept. of Sociology, University of Surrey 1979), p. 73.

5 *National Catholic Reporter*, 3 July 1981.

6 For the history of the Sword/CIIR see Michael Walsh, *From Swords to Ploughshares* (CIIR 1980).

7 Diocese of Westminster, East London Area, *Report of Area Pastoral Assembly*, 22 February 1981, p. 5.

8 G. A. Beck, ed., *The English Catholics 1850-1950* (Burns Oates 1950), p. 604.

9 Hornsby-Smith and Lee, op. cit., pp. 37-9.

10 ibid, pp. 125-6.

11 cf. Patrick Jenkin on Credo, LWT, 11 May 1980.

12 cf. M. Kerr, *The People of Ship Street* (Routledge & Kegan Paul 1958).

13 Jeffrey K. Hadden, *The Gathering Storm in the Churches: A Sociologist's View of the Widening Gap Between Clergy and Laymen* (New York, Doubleday, 1969).

14 David Nicholls in K. Leech, ed., *Christianity Reinterpreted?* (Church in Wales Publications 1979).

5

Authority and the Bishop in the Church

Rowan Williams

1

If I say that I am 'under authority', what am I asserting about myself? The centurion in the gospel,[1] when he thus describes himself, is saying that he understands what it means to act freely so as to affect the fate of someone else in a decisive fashion, establishing certain things and excluding others, because he himself is so 'affected' by others and is in turn authorized to 'affect' those committed to his charge. 'I am under authority' means – among other things – 'I am not the sole maker of my world; my possibilities are limited.' Authority, in the most basic sense, has to do with precisely this limiting of options: authoritative phenomena (they need not always be verbal pronouncements: we can sensibly talk about 'authoritative' readings or performances of musical and dramatic works) provide a sharpening of definition which, explicitly or implicitly, points up areas of conflict and possible exclusion. Even in the aesthetic area, if I say that I find Grigory Kosintsev's film of *King Lear* an 'authoritative' version of Shakespeare's play, I am accepting that there are ways of reading the play that are now ruled out, or at least relativized, questioned or overshadowed, by Kosintsev's – as far as I am concerned. To use another kind of image, what is 'authoritative' clarifies the distinction between the essential and the peripheral, and persuades me of the superior *significance* of certain features of the subject

90

matter. Not all interpretations are of equal validity; not all are equally possible for me, therefore, once I have grasped some one interpretation as authoritative.

So to talk about authority as something which limits possibilities is to see it as *giving definition*. At the simplest level, to give an order to another person is to impose definition on his or her actions, to shape their future this way or that. And it is quite right to say, as the late Yves Simon does in his lucid monograph on the idea of authority,[2] that a great deal of the exercise of authority in the average human society is necessarily 'arbitrary', in that it defines the legitimate limits of citizens' options on matters without any intrinsic significance (which side of the road we drive on, for instance). The significant reason for which one course of action rather than another is enjoined has nothing to do with any aspect of the action as such; it relates entirely to the desirability – in some circumstances, the practical necessity – of a common order for the sake of the common good. A state may allow theoretical freedom of conscience to its citizens as to which side of the road it is *better* to drive on, but even the most minimal grasp of the idea of 'common good' suggests that this freedom has to be severely limited in practice.

But of course authority in society is not uniformly like that. In indifferent matters, it does not much matter by what means authority is actually exercised, so long as there is some mechanism for the making of decisions. Other considerations arise when what is being 'defined' does have a significance of its own. Societies as they actually exist define 'the common good' in specific (and therefore arguable, controversial) terms; they operate with more or less explicit assumptions about what human welfare, harmony and fulfilment look like. Now in their attempt to achieve a closer approximation to their vision, they will necessarily take decisions which require for their implementation that certain human habits and attitudes can be relied on; and the problem comes when these habits and attitudes that are taken for granted are directly in conflict with the overall human goals of the group. That is to say, if a society professes a commitment to participatory democracy and yet (in supposed defence of this ideal) organizes itself in a way that effectively disfranchises the mass of its population, its actual exercise of authority is impeding and not furthering its goals. The irony of a 'free world' putatively defended by nuclear weaponry is a case in point: nuclear policy has (at least until very recently) been conspicuously inattentive to the question of how far it is answerable to the community it purports to defend, and many would argue that the exercise of political authority in societies thus armed is inescapably undemocratic. Similar points could be made about a 'free' society which effectively took (takes?) for granted a situation of 'structural unemployment' in its exercise of authority in the economic realm.

But these are issues which would demand far more discussion to do them justice. The point is that any method of exercising authority which runs counter to the professed goals of a group is subversive of its own credibility: it is a lot harder to take seriously a society's claim to stand for liberty and co-operation if those values are not witnessed to in its present practice of government. And this very soon generates in such a society a profound disillusion – the loss of any sense of a moral significance inhering in the life of the community, and the decay of *corporate* life and enterprise. Means and ends are in fact far less easily separable in the political world than we are sometimes led to believe.[3]

2

Why spend so long in a theological essay on matters that may seem more properly to belong in political philosophy? Partly because 'authority' is, whether we like it or not, a political concept as soon as it is applied to the life of *any* community, and it may help us if we clarify in advance some of the dilemmas which arise in connection with it. Christians are liable to a certain naiveté (sometimes genuine, sometimes feigned) about the nature and exercise of power. It is perfectly true that power and authority are not identical;[4] yet the common life of human beings involves authority, defining and limiting authority, being exercised, and this will involve reflection on means and ends, and so, inevitably, reflection on the appropriate use of power. It is naive (on the one hand) to say that the Church does not have anything to do with 'power';[5] and it is potentially disastrous to say (on the other) that the actual way authority works is peripheral – if the sacramental life of Christians, their sanctification in prayer and love, is going on, it doesn't really matter how the Church is organized. This is a *very* tempting viewpoint, especially for those quite reasonably exasperated by the institutional immobility of various Christian communions; but unfortunately it does bypass the question of means and ends. And it is capable of producing among Christians exactly the same sense of a 'loss of moral significance' in the life of the Church as large as occurs in secular society. The retreat into the Small Group is a simple solution, but one which runs against all that the idea of 'catholicity' has positively meant in the Church: the mutual critical openness of the local body and the wider structure, the reciprocal nourishment offered by particular local communities. And if catholicity matters, structures of authority matter.

The Church, as a community of human beings struggling to realize a particular vision of human welfare, harmony and fulfilment, requires that there be some way in which options can be made as to whether or not certain acts or styles of life are compatible with its vision, and some point at which clearer focusing of its goals is possible. It requires authority; but because of the nature of its goals, it requires authority of a particular kind, whose exercise is discernibly in tune with those goals, nurturing the humanity that is sought for. In all this, of course, there is nothing uniquely 'churchly'; it is only as we begin to consider more particularly the nature of the Christian goal or vision that what is distinctive about Christian authority can begin to emerge.

3

The Christian gospel affirms that forgiveness occurs: people responsible for the hurt and diminution of others are not condemned to permanent lostness. If they own their acts in seriousness and in desire to do otherwise (in penitence), they are set free to belong to a community in which the constitutive reality is mutual gift and enrichment. The pivot of this self-recognition, this liberation and this new corporate life, the event which makes all this possible, is the 'paschal mystery' of the death and exaltation of Jesus: God's blameless servant is the victim of a paradigmatic act of violence and rejection, but God 'returns' him to the world as the ultimate and decisive symbol of undefeated compassion and inexhaustible creative resource. Upon this gift hangs the possibility of the existence of a shared life of gift: that is what the Church is created and constituted to be.

So the 'goals' of the Church can be described in terms of the formation of a human community in which oppressive and diminishing relationships are transformed through the mediation of a controlling story or image. The human options available to the Church are limited by the force of this central symbol: cross and resurrection constitute an *authoritative* reality in the believing community. The Church's limits are defined at the most primary level by its reference to an event in which violent power is judged and grace and mutuality are declared to be the fundamental ways in which God lives and is shown in the world. The Church's gospel speaks of a transformation effected by recognition, 'confession' in both senses of the word: the acknowledgement of responsibility, and the acknowledgement of a firm commitment and trust; it is an invitation to *see*, and so depends upon a basic metaphor of unveiling and showing. In the Fourth Gospel, this is spelled out in the pervasive account of Jesus' presence in the world and the Church as 'light'; in

Paul and the Letter to the Ephesians (whether Paul's or not, it is in this respect perceptibly a development of his characteristic concerns), the recurring language of the opening and revealing of the *mysterion* of God's plan serves a similar purpose.

'Showing' is an effective, catalytic and transforming event, which draws new boundaries. That is to say, it is an authoritative event, yet also one which, in demanding responsible choice, implies that its authority cannot be coercively exercised. And to belong to the Christian community is to accept the paschal symbol as decisive: a showing of truth which challenges and involves, demands response, and is generative of new life, individual and corporate. From the beginning, acceptance of the gospel has not formally involved any act of submission to an administrative structure, but has taken the form of incorporation into a worshipping – a ritual-celebrating – group by means of an enactment of the Easter symbol in baptism: immersion and emergence, loss and recovery, death and life. And the act which both expresses and fosters the community's coherence is again a ritual recovery of Easter (however much in its history it has been distorted into a recollection only of the cross): new life as gift, in the regular and repeated nourishment of a meal.

4

If this is true, the simplest and most central 'authority' in the Church is this authority of the *symbol*. It is a kind of authority connected intimately with the human goals of the Church in that those goals involve response and self-awareness and are *not* served by the abandonment of the capacity for freedom and discrimination. 'Obedience' to a symbol is a very different matter from obedience to a command. 'We are saved by Christ's obedience not because it was blind but . . . because it was unswerving and total response to perceived truth';[6] and that obedience itself becomes the symbol we must likewise obey. It is 'perceived truth' for us, and demands a response of like order, and like cost. To treat Christian obedience as a *sacrificium intellectus* is to trivialize it: the cost is deeper. There may have to be obedience to the paschal symbol when clarity and security, 'understanding' at the ordinary level, are all missing; but this depends on the basic trust that even this darkness in the symbol is fertile and creative, not upon a deliberate suspension of judgement and responsibility.[7]

What limits our options is the symbol accepted as definitive. But we are not speaking of a static material symbol (Christians do not possess a Qur'an), rather of symbolic acts performed in particular historical communities of men and women. Baptism and the Eucharist do not happen independently of a tradition of their performance, passed on in a personal fashion; and they are 'orchestrated' in one way or another according to a wide variety of social and ideological constraints. Thus the authority of our baptismal and eucharistic symbols is actually encountered in a variety of practical ways, dependent upon the variety of people engaged in their celebration.

If this is so, it is both sociologically and theologically intelligible that the *persons* believed to exercise authority in the Church are those engaged most directly in the enactment of its symbols: the teaching authority of the bishop (or his delegate) is, in the early Church, inseparable from his role as eucharistic president. 'His primary function is always to *make the catholicity of the Church reveal itself in a certain place*',[8] by being the focal point around which the community gathers, overcoming its divisions, to affirm a single identity governed by the paschal symbol in its eucharistic shape – 'catholicity' here being seen as the incorporation of the many into the one, the individual into the communal, the local into the universal.[9] If authority belongs primarily to the symbol, it belongs derivatively to whoever gives that symbol concrete and coherent form. In early Christian practice, *only* the bishop baptized, just as only the bishop ordained, because it is only by reference to the single figure in a district set apart to be *himself* a 'symbol' accessible to all, related to all, not representing only a sector of the community, that the actual limits of the Church can be discerned. Pragmatically, the Church was those who assembled round the bishop, those recognized by the bishop as having placed their lives under the authority of the crucified and risen Jesus.

5

But there is an obvious trap here (into which the Church has generally fallen). It is to see the sacramental authority of the bishop as that of the mystagogue, to whom is entrusted 'guardianship' of the sacred things; and the succession of ministerial order in terms of the passing-on of powers or prerogatives closed off to the rest of the community. Here authority depends upon the ability to manipulate symbolic language professionally: the symbol is the possession of, or at least the deposit entrusted to, a class in the Church. Thus authority comes to be seen as *rule* exercised by a 'teaching' body over a passive 'learning' body – *ecclesia docens* and *ecclesia discens*, the empowered and initiated over against the uninstructed.

But this is to make a nonsense of the role of the symbol itself. Precisely because we are speaking of a *common* symbol (the paschal event) which governs and unifies the whole community, there can be no mystagogic view of the minister lifting the veil from secrets hidden from the eyes of the multitude, by virtue of initiation into a privileged sacral caste. The paschal symbol is what brings the whole Church into being and draws multiple identities into a common one. In its ritual, the *whole* Church shows itself its source and its criterion; but no particular act of showing is of the same creative order as the paschal event itself, so that no act of showing has meaning independently of the generative event and the life of the community as a whole. That is, we do not have to do, in the sacraments, with a *series* of theophanies presented to a passive audience. In the rather different language of Reformation controversy, there cannot be several sacrifices, repeated sacrifices, of Christ; because the community that celebrates is unified by reference to the one sacrifice, the one symbol, whose uniqueness is guaranteed by its historical particularity. The paschal mystery is indeed, in the Church, an 'open secret'.

So there can be no class of 'initiates' (the early Church rightly referred to *all* its baptized as *mystai*, initiates); an authority exercised by such a class over the rest of the Church would be subversive of the real authority of the symbol it claimed to safeguard, and thus, in undermining the symbolic mode of authority and the symbolic mode of obedience, would also subvert the human goals of the Church. Invitation and manifestation would be replaced by the inevitable domination of the instructed over the uninstructed: a class of permanently 'deprived' persons would be built into the Church, persons whose converted self-awareness could be mediated only by way of the expertise of the professional handler and performer of the symbolic. It is no surprise, then, if a revival of the corporate sense of the Eucharist goes hand in hand with a re-examination of the structures of clerical authority: or if the former fails to be realized (whatever the favoured rhetoric may be) when the latter lags behind.

In what sense, then, do we speak of the authority of the bishop-as-liturgist? Certainly if symbolic authority is primary in the Church, there cannot properly be forms of authority radically divorced from the sacramental context; but what does this mean in practice? If the bishop's function is essentially to enable the community to state in ritual form its unity in the crucified and risen Christ (and thus also its freedom from exclusively local prejudice and interest – its catholicity), he does not speak or teach 'authoritatively' in abstraction from the community at worship. 'There is no ministry in the catholic Church that can exist *in absoluto*.'[10] And in the context of the community at worship, his speaking, teaching or acting must be intrinsically part of a shared exploration into the Church's common identity. He may be focus or *animateur* of liturgy, but he cannot be a virtuoso soloist. The nature of his eucharistic role obliges him to be ministered *to*, to be nourished by the understanding of all. And his task is then to interpret these ministries, these contributions back to the Church, and to interpret different sectors to each other; to manifest to the Church its own multiplicity of ways of apprehending and responding to its governing symbol.

The bishop's authority, in other words, is an authority to unify: not an authority to abolish or minimize conflict within the community, but the task of referring all sides of a debate to the unifying symbol over whose ritual recollection he presides, in such a way as to show the face of strangers or opponents in the Church as Christ's face for each other. This means he also has the task of discriminating – of judging when some response to the gospel is incapable of being Christ's face. This involves no small risk, but it is one thing which saves such an exercise of authority from blandness: nothing can be gained by attempting to interpret as Christ's the face of naked racialism, militarism, or any comparable phenomenon which is of its essence opposed to the human goals of the Church.

Thus authority in the Church can operate positively when a bishop says to one group: 'Your opponents are also "in my communion". I recognize them as baptized, as having confessed Jesus as Lord, and I do so for such-and-such reasons. Listen to them, as they must to you. When you rupture your fellowship with them, you rupture your fellowship with me at the Lord's table.' Equally it can operate (less often, we may hope) negatively, if a bishop says to the community at large: 'Such-and-such a group has broken the fellowship of Christ's table by its attitudes, and I cannot see how it confesses Christ.' This is not necessarily to plead for the renewal of the discipline of excommunication (which is fraught with ambiguities) but at least to demand of communities and dissident groups within them that they examine with candour whether their professed unity is *really* a common obedience to the paschal symbol.

In this way, the bishop's authoritative role is to realize in the community he serves the ultimate significance of those patterns of mutuality, 'the rejection of rejection', gift and acceptance which are meant to characterize the body of believers in Jesus: it is for him to show how the face of the stranger can be a gift and not a menace within the Church. His exercise of authority, in manner and context, must serve the creation and growth of that community of gift which is God's purpose for the humanity made in his image. And the bishop is equipped to do this because he is 'put there' by the Church to focus its unity in presiding at the common meal. At this level, he is (as we have noted) himself a symbol. He does not have power over the community, far less power over the symbol; rather he becomes part of the symbolic mediation by which the Church renews its encounter with what creates it and sustains it – the grace of Christ. And anything that needs to be said about succession, legitimation, continuity of tradition, and so forth must be spelled out in relation to this symbolic sense of ministerial order: if a bishop is truly to unveil the catholicity of the local church, he cannot depend for his ordination only on the local and the contemporary, he must visibly belong in a community extended in time and space beyond the local. But exactly what 'conditions' should be specified for this is not my immediate concern here.

6

Now by this time, some exasperated readers may want to ask, '*What* church are you talking about? and what bishops? These models may be very interesting in their way, but how do they relate to the present structures of any real church?' This is fair enough: my 'bishop' may indeed be such a creature as never was on sea or land. But there is a place for sorting out a little what the inner coherences of the Church's life involve, what sorts of ministry most clearly belong with the professed purposes of the Church's existence, if only to prevent our assuming that whatever form of ministerial authority we presently have is un-criticizable, or that any form of authority which works must be defensible. In other words, I am reiterating a plea often made, that theology should have a properly *critical* role in the Church's view of itself. Its job is not to be merely descriptive.

It is true, though, that when we think of authority in the Church, we think first of the way it is actually exercised now in various Christian communions. Even those Eastern Orthodox writers who have done most to clarify the liturgical and symbolic basis of episcopal authority would admit that their account is by no means instantly recog-nizable in the present practice of their own churches. Yet it remains largely true that the Orthodox (and the non-Byzantine Eastern Churches) have felt less need than any other Christian body for structures of decision-making at a level other than the local,[11] and will still wax eloquently abusive about the un-catholic character of a putatively universal authority.[12] Is it sufficient to say that the 'local' church (and it is of course far from straightforward to define the limits of the local) should remit to its bishop (or, conceivably, a small group of bishops chaired by a 'metro-politan') the responsibility for policy-making in the Christian community, and not look for any wider or firmer ground of authority than the assurance that the bishop is recognized by his brothers in the episcopate?

Primitivist solutions are always seductive. But a complex and mobile society forbids us to rest content with this episcopal version of the Small Group ideology. When the Church exists in a wide variety of social situations, then, if we take seriously the understanding of catholicity as the transcending of the local and the idea of the Church as a community of mutual gift, the local church's representative must be actively and regularly engaged in interpreting his church to other churches, and vice versa. Of course this has always been understood to be part of the bishop's job; my point is that as the social and cultural diversity of Christians grows more marked, the interpretative gifts required demand far more regular and consistent exercise and education than ever before.[13] In the early and medieval periods, the problem tended to be resolved by the relative cultural homogeneity of ecclesiastical bodies, confirmed by schisms whose roots were as much cultural as theological. Western Christendom had its common ground in the Latin tongue and the authority of the Curia; Eastern Orthodoxy in the political ambience of the Imperial Court, and a kind of Byzantine political-ideological-aesthetic vernacular; non-Chalcedonian Christianity (not that it faced grave problems of policy and doctrine in this period) in the common social situation of a religio-ethnic minority under Muslim rule.

Within these circles, the bishop's interpretative work does not involve the demanding cross-cultural translations of a more pluralist situation. But in the later kind of situation, the bishop's unifying authority *within* a community will depend in large measure on his sensitivity to the range of Christian options in the world at large, and thus upon his interpretative skills in this wider context. Hence the need for structures which permit precisely this kind of exchange, and which nurture and preserve a 'catholic' perspective in the bishop's mind, enabling him, *inter alia*, to speak more clearly and powerfully on behalf of strangers and minorities within his own community.

But if this is true, any 'consultative' structures set up to facilitate this are not going to be in themselves authoritative organs of decision-making. They are there to *serve* the authority of the bishop as 'catholic' representative in the local church, in his own sphere of action, and in no sense to impose decisions upon him. They may remind him that to preserve his (and his community's) openness to the wider life of the Church, he cannot act with a degree of independence that merely reflects an insensitivity to other attitudes and practices; but they are not there actively to inhibit him, let alone to make policy for him. If a structure which (necessarily) exists at some distance from particular worshipping communities conceives itself to have a directive authority, it shows a misunderstanding of the sources of Christian authority. So that (to give, for once, a concrete and familiar instance) the Lambeth Conference is entirely right not to promulgate binding decisions but to concentrate upon the formation of general attitudes and perspectives. There are various ways of securing this kind of 'catholic' exchange in the service of a genuinely unifying authority at the local level, and it is immensely encouraging to see how the Anglican Communion is developing more channels for such encounters.

7

What then about the processes of decision-making in the local context? There is no obvious reason why a bishop should be involved in any and every administrative mechanism relating to the church in his district; but decisions and policies which affect the Church's understanding of its boundaries and its goals will obviously require his engagement *if* the Church is conscious of being essentially a liturgical community (a community that utters, celebrates and symbolizes what it is). We have already seen that his authority is meaningless independently of what is actually happening and being said; so that it is pretty well superfluous to underline that he cannot properly act in an individualistic way. And again, this requires the development of structures, more or less sophisticated, which guard against his exercising an authority *over* the Church.

Here we encounter some very vexed questions indeed. Synodical government in the Church of England was created largely to provide just such a safeguard, to ensure that authority was exercised in a corporate, participatory style. The problem is that, as presently practised, it is heavily dependent upon a model of a 'parliamentary' kind; members represent constituencies, organize themselves in blocs, legislate by majority vote, and vote by 'houses'. All of this is (fairly) administratively tidy; but it is theologically untidy. It is reasonable that in a diocesan synod there should be represented both regional and 'partisan' interests, but it seems to me more questionable whether the present method of elections contested between candidates offering quasi-legislative programmes is the healthiest way of proceeding. Naturally, so long as a synod is seen as essentially a legislative body, it is inevitable that its membership should be relatively large in order to secure effective representation. But should it be? And when we come to consider the General Synod of the Church of England, the anomalies seem still sharper: it is a synod of two provinces, increasingly conscious of and jealous of its legislative powers; it is also expected to be a consultative forum for the discussion of complex ethical and theological matters. In the terms of this essay's thesis, its authority is hard to locate in relation to the Church as worshipping community. It is desirable, certainly, to have some procedures in the Church for the settling of questions of canonical regularity, but I am still a little unconvinced by the parliamentary analogy ('no taxation without representation'). Smaller groups, more regionally based, might be capable of co-ordination and, if necessary, 'codifying' disciplinary policy; and the 'consultative forum' aspect of a synod's work could be freed from the legislative aspect – which would allow some rethinking on appropriate kinds of representation, and, above all, on the strange practice of voting by houses (as if bishops, other ranks, and laity were clearly defined 'interest groups'), which does little to speak for the kind of genuinely corporate authority synodical government is meant to guarantee.

As for the diocesan level: can we imagine a situation in which a bishop (and perhaps a small body of consultants) actually formed part of *several* local policy-forming groups? This would at least underline the primacy of concrete local communities in working out their decisions for their own life, in the presence of and with the aid of the 'catholic', the connecting, bridge-building, figure of the bishop. And to the objection that this would add intolerable burdens to the episcopal work-load, the simple reply is to invite serious reconsideration of the average size of the diocese. I am all too well aware that the 'bishop' of this essay, as focus for a regional community, is a fiction in the present situation of territorially enormous dioceses. The 'episcopal' function I have been trying to describe is in *fact* exercised by a variety of figures, including area deans and team rectors (the best account of *episkope* I have heard came from the vicar of a very large and variegated city centre parish, with a multiplicity of house groups, describing his work as a co-ordinator of existing ministries); and that may provide some food for thought.

All of this is speculative kite-flying, of course; but I am profoundly concerned that the way authority is actually exercised in the Church should have some degree of answerability to the specific nature of the Church as a community – that it should, in other words, be open to theological critiques. This essay has suggested certain grounds for criticism, but there are many other possible starting points. Not all would concur in my suspicions of centralized authority and representative legislature. And there remains one very important area of discussion related to this, which has to do with the kind of co-ordination appropriate between the plurality of church communities clustered around their *episkopoi*. Is there anything which 'holds the ring' for the ensemble of these communities, as a touchstone of catholicity? which is, in effect, to raise the question of *papacy*.

8

The Petrine office is regularly said to be to the whole Church what the bishop is in the local community: the interpreter of each to all, the focal point of unity. And the Roman Catholic is entitled to ask those outside the papal fold (in the light of the none-too-encouraging history of Protestantism and of Eastern Christianity) how effective unity, authentically free exchange and communication and *communion*, can ever be realized without such a symbol, drawing the many into the one. Further, if the bishop's role as symbol of unity defines his authority as authority to unify, the same is true of the Pope: in the Church at large, the Pope's task is to refer all Christians to the single catholic truth, the paschal symbol.

This seems plausible (and it is, I think, quite close to what the 1977 ARCIC Report on *Authority in the Church* says about the papacy); but here are still some unresolved problems I should like to air. The first and most obvious is this: the bishop's role in the community derives from his sacramental function as the one around whom the assembly gathers to celebrate; in what sense could anything comparable be said of the Pope? He is, in fact, bishop of a particular church, he is not without a sacramental role: but does he have a sacramental role vis-à-vis *all* the churches? Is this not in fact to risk de-catholicizing the local church as such, by implying that the *true* bishop of every church is the Pope (and Vatican I came very near to saying just that)? The problem is of course intensified by the heavily juridical imagery used since the early Middle Ages to describe the papal office, the Church being conceived as the domain in which the Pope is supreme magistrate.[14]

Various points might be made in reply. For instance, we might say that the real focus of unity is the church of the prime apostles, the Roman community that assembled first around the apostles of the circumcision and the uncircumcision, the first and the last witnesses of the risen Jesus. This is a community which, historically, acts as a sort of classical model for others: it is a paradigm assembly around the witnesses of the resurrection, a model of a community identifying itself through the paschal event. And so it makes sense to say that, derivatively, its bishop has a symbolic and paradigmatic role for all 'episcopal' assemblies.[15] Or the related point might be made that, if the most primitive assembly was gathered after Easter around Peter, when he had been 'converted' and restored by the risen Jesus,[16] if Peter was indeed the foundation stone upon which the Church was established, then Peter's church and Peter's successor have the same status: now as then, the catholic Church is the church assembled round Peter.

Both these are serious theological proposals. The second, more specific, argument seems to me the more questionable, since it could be said that *every* bishop 'inherits' a Petrine role in this sense, and that anyway it is question-begging to think of one church, let alone one bishop, somehow repeating or continuing the work of the first apostle at Easter. The former and looser argument seems roughly to tie in with a good deal of what the Fathers of the first four centuries say about Rome (it is certainly worth stressing that Peter and Paul are equally important for such writers), and I suspect there may be more mileage in it. But on *either* showing, the corollaries fall short of a strictly 'papalist' view of authority. Neither argument gives any basis for supposing that the Pope has an authority definable in individual terms (any more than any bishop has), let alone that local bishops in any way derive authority from him. He in his church should show what episcopal authority ought to be in a community, because that community (for various reasons) began as a paradigm 'community of resurrection', drawing its sense of identity from the two great witnesses. And ideally (we could go on to say), just as decisions locally are not made without the bishop, the liturgical president, reflection in the Church at large on its nature and destiny should not be done without the Roman bishop. I have carefully avoided speaking of 'decision' in the Church at large, however, because (as I argued earlier on) supra-local structures should not be seen as basically decision-making bodies for the whole Church, even if, in exceptional circumstances, they may temporarily become so. Thus the papacy could be an indispensable sign of the true catholicity consultative (not legislative) structures in the Church: a 'council' which ignored the bishop of Rome would be an extremely suspect assembly – and again, patristic analogies could be adduced for some such formulation.

Once again, this is speculative. I think, though, that it is important to engage seriously with a theology of 'Petrine office' (allowing that it directs some pertinent criticism against, say, the purely pragmatic federalism of the Anglican Communion) but also to challenge the pervasively individualistic and unsacramental ways in which this office and its authority have been conceived. We need to subject to a rigorous critique the apparently unmodified commitment in the Roman Catholic Church to a belief in the symbolic uniqueness of the papacy in the Church's life, the insistence upon an individual charism different in kind from that of other bishops. The 'infallibilist' problem is still very far from a satisfactory resolution in the dialogue not only between Anglicans and Roman Catholics but also between the Orthodox (and non-Byzantine Eastern) Churches and Rome.

9

To sum up then: I have tried to argue (i) that the exercise of authority in any human society is without credibility if it frustrates the overall directing aim or vision of human life by which the society professed to live; (ii) that the primary source of authority in the Christian Church is a controlling symbol, liturgically appropriated, which speaks of the recovery of a self-aware responsiveness and the transformation of mutual threat into mutual gift: (iii) that it therefore makes sense to see authoritative decision-making in the Christian community as exercised by the worshipping group gathered around the symbolic figure of the liturgical president (the 'bishop' – in practice, often, the delegates of the bishop); (iv) that this specifies for the bishop a kind of authority which consists in *interpretation*, and the presentation as far as possible of mutual openness in the Church; and (v) that non-local structures in the Church should see their *primary* role as enriching this local exercise of authority. Thus the bishop does not make decisions, doctrinal or disciplinary, alone: the Church decides, and the bishop's unique role is to guarantee that *all* the Church decides. And this led us to make some critical points about various non-local 'authorities', and to try to see how they might serve rather than dominate the local church.

Authority in the Church should constantly return us to our common authoritative symbol, to a contemplative receptivity to its challenge and its judgement. That symbol, I have said, is normally renewed for us in worship. But this is not to say that the symbol is only renewed here: John Drury points out[17] that, 'Authority in the church has been exercised by Kierkegaard who ostentatiously sat in his club on Sunday mornings; by the lonely, ecclesiastically un-assimilated figure of Charles Péguy; and by Simone Weil who doggedly and articulately refused baptism.' Receptivity to the symbol can involve us in hearing its judgement from those who are marginal to the Church's symbolic life – who are, rather, *marginalized* by the Church's failure to be what it sacramentally says it is, the community of gift. But we can only see such figures as authoritative if we already know and feel the contours of the paschal symbol from elsewhere – from the 'ordinary' life of the baptizing and eucharistizing community. The refusal of baptism can only be a significant deepening of our symbolic awareness if there is a residue of significance and integrity *in* the baptismal rite itself which enables us to see that in certain circumstances a person who turns away from baptism shows us *more* of what baptism symbolizes than the person whose reception of the rite is unreflective. Simone Weil speaks more authoritatively than many of the *cost* of self-loss and self-recovery.

Yet this is also to say that to speak of the authority of a Kierkegaard or a Simone Weil in abstraction from the abiding centrality of sacramental life in community is merely romantic: the 'authority' of heroic integrity alone provides no substantial basis for a Christian view of authority. The great isolated figures of Christian history are answerable to the same symbol we are all answerable to, and their stature is assessed by reference to that. Otherwise we have a multitude of 'Vatican I' popes, not answerable to the Church at large; and it is important to note that the conspicuous absence in Kierkegaard and Simone Weil (Péguy is a very different case) of any theology of communion and interdependence is bound to qualify anything we say about their authority '*in* the Church'.

So we come back to the fundamental point of this essay: authority in the Church cannot straightforwardly be exercised by an individual 'over' a group. Understanding what fruitful patterns of Christian authority might look like has to do with understanding what is involved in loyalty or obedience to the symbol, the story, displayed to all: 'Jesus Christ . . . publicly portrayed as crucified' (Gal. 3.1). Authority in the Church is the re-presenting, the lifting up of the Son of man reigning exalted from his cross, in word, life, and sign; its strength will always be in its fidelity to that, even (or especially?) when the lifting-up is the inarticulate or muddled or unpersuasive insistent childlike *pointing* of which Paul seems to speak. 'I decided to know nothing among you except Jesus Christ and him crucified. And I was with you in weakness and in much fear and trembling; and my speech and my message were not in plausible words of wisdom, but in demonstration of the Spirit of power, that your faith might not rest in the wisdom of men but in the power of God' (1 Cor. 2. 2–5).

NOTES

1 Matt. 8.8; Luke 7.8.

2 *A General Theory of Authority*, (2nd edn, with a new introduction by Vukan Kuic), University of Notre Dame Press, 1980); see, e.g., pp. 40–41, 43–47.

3 It is a weakness in Simon's argument that he rather underrates this dimension of the problem by assuming tacitly

that the means of securing unanimity in areas where there is a legitimate plurality of 'good ends' is not of primary moral concern.

4   See, e.g., R. Murray SJ, 'Authority and the Spirit in the New Testament', in R. Murray and others, *Authority in a Changing Church* (London, DLT, 1968), and the discussion of this paper in Nicholas Lash's *Voices of Authority* (London, Sheed and Ward, 1976), ch. 2, pp. 17–24.

5   The declaration made by the Taizé 'Concile des jeunes' in 1971, demanding a Church 'stripped of the means of power', reflects a characteristic unclarity in this matter.

6   Nicholas Lash, op. cit., p. 112.

7   ibid.

8   John Zizioulas, 'The Eucharistic Community and the Catholicity of the Church' (a seminally important essay), in John Meyendorff and Joseph McLelland, ed., *The New Man: An Orthodox and Reformed Dialogue* (New York, Agora Books, 1973), p. 128 (italics in original); this essay first appeared in *One in Christ*, 2–3, 1971.

9   ibid., p. 127.

10 ibid. p. 128; cf. the argument of Edward Schillebeeckx in *Ministry. A case for change* (London, SCM, 1981), a work to which I am much indebted.

11 There is some valuable discussion of the historical and contemporary role of General Councils in Eastern Orthodoxy in John Meyendorff's paper, 'What is an Ecumenical Council?', reproduced in his *Living Tradition: Orthodox Witness in the Contemporary World* (New York, St Vladimir's Seminary Press, 1978), esp. pp. 58–62.

12 As in Archimandrite Vasilios (Basile) of Stavronikita, *Chant d'entrée. Vie liturgique et mystère de l'unité dans l'Église Orthodoxe* (Geneva, Labor et Fides, 1980), pp. 47–56.

13 It is in this connection that we should view the recent creation of an Anglican Maori diocese in the Province of New Zealand – as a response to the need of a particular cultural group for 'interpretation' to the wider community, in a situation where the integrity and self-valuing of the sub-group is at a critical stage of articulation.

14 See the detailed treatment of this in W. Ullmann, *Mediaeval Political Thought* (London, Pelican Books, 1979: originally *A History of Political Thought: the Middle Ages*, London, Pelican Books, 1965 and 1970), esp. ch. 1.

15 This is discussed most illuminatingly, with particular reference to the ambiguities of Vatican I, in Roland Minnerath, *Le Pape. Évêque universel ou premier des évêques* (Paris, Beauchesne, 1978), esp. chs. 3 and 4. I am indebted to the Reverend Christopher Hill for drawing my attention to this work.

The final statement of ARCIC (Windsor 1981), *Authority in the Church II*, appeared too late to be referred to in the body of this essay. It is notable that here the discussion of primacy appears to be carried on with rather limited reference to the Pope's position as bishop in a *particular* church; nevertheless, it makes it quite clear that the Pope is a member of the episcopal order (para. 11). Given this, it is odd to see so sharp a distinction drawn between the 'universal primate' and the 'diocesan bishop . . . *subject to his authority*' (para. 20; my italics), even when this authority is held to be *jure divino* only when exercised in some sort of 'collegiality' with other bishops.

16 This approach has most recently been restated, very cogently, in Edward Schillebeeckx, *Jesus. An Experiment in Christology* (London, Collins, 1979), pp. 388–90.

17 In his editorial in *Theology*, May 1977, p. 162.

6
Structures for Unity

John Macquarrie

'It is a well known fact,' writes Leszek Kolakowski,'to which the history of civilization records no exception, that all important ideas are subject to division and differentiation as their influence continues to spread.'[1] This generalization, which Kolakowski applies to the history of Marxism, holds equally for Christianity. In the course of its development, it has taken many forms in order to address itself to different cultures, different individual types and different needs. The capacity for differentiation is an evidence and a tribute to the fruitfulness, importance and power for renewal that from the beginning have characterized the movement springing from Christ and the apostles.

In large measure, this process of differentiation has been beneficial. The rich content of Christianity has been increasingly unpacked, its adaptability to different cultural contexts has been demonstrated, its appeal to all sorts and conditions of human beings has become clear. But like all other historical developments, this one has its ambiguities. Because of human sin, differentiation has hardened into faction, strife, rivalry, bitterness and separation. What might have been a richly differentiated community, embracing within itself the contributions of many interpretations, vocations and life styles, has broken up into a large number of communities, some of them quite hostile to each other.

But the evil consequences of division and separation should not blind us to the benefits that have accrued

113

through differentiation as a necessary condition for the outreach of the Christian message to the many types of human beings. Historical differentiation of this kind is, in any case, irreversible. So whatever structures of unity we envisage to heal those breaches that have occurred in the Christian Church, we shall have to be careful to ensure that whatever is valuable in the different forms is preserved and given scope for further development in the reconstituted whole. In other words, we must aim at a pluralist Church (I shall say more in a moment about the meaning of 'pluralism'). The unity of the Church *after* the irreversible process of differentiation has taken place cannot be the same as its unity *before* that process began. Indeed, if there ever was an undifferentiated unity in the Church, it must have been of very short duration, for even in the New Testament one can distinguish different types of churches. In this respect, the birth of the Christian Church could be compared to the hypothetical 'big bang' at the beginning of the universe – it began forthwith to expand in every direction, and as it did so, it exhibited different possibilities and developed different forms.

Let me come back to the word 'pluralism', for some Christians seem to be afraid of it when it is applied to the Church. Certainly, we more often apply it to the secular state. In the world today, pluralism is the mark of mature societies, and by that we mean that in such societies there is the maximum of freedom for individuals and groups to engage in such activities and adopt such life styles as will best develop their personal endowments. Of course, such pluralism has to be compatible with the cohesion of the society concerned. On the other hand, societies that are immature, backward, oppressive and insecure try to conform their citizens to a single pattern through one-party political systems, state-controlled schools and universities, censorship of the media and so on. The danger of the pluralist state is that individual and group freedoms may be pushed to the point where they threaten the stability of the society as a whole. So at that point there emerges the very difficult question of how one reconciles unity with diversity, a common allegiance with individual and group liberty.

Parallel problems present themselves in matters ecclesiastical and constitute one of the major difficulties for contemporary ecumenism. It is generally recognized that the age of monolithic churches is passing, if it has not already passed. There have been churches that have sought to impose uniformity in doctrine, liturgy and moral conduct and that developed the authoritarian structures needed to enforce such uniformity. But it is now generally conceded that some measure of pluralism is justified. This is apparent in the area of liturgy, where liturgical revision now provides even alternative canons of the Mass. In matters of doctrine, Karl Rahner has acknowledged that there will be a plurality of theologies, though he is careful to point out that these will not contradict one another, though they will be incapable of synthesis because of their different philosophical idioms.[2] The same writer has also claimed that in moral theology the Church will leave more to the discrimination of the individual.[3] Yet there must be limits to such pluralism. However difficult it may be to say where these limits lie, it has been recognized from New Testament times onward that either in doctrine or practice one may stray so far from the mainstream of the Christian community that one ends up outside.

Perhaps partly due to the growing recognition of the virtues of pluralism, perhaps partly due to the failure of many national and regional 'schemes' of union, there has been in recent years a decisive shift in thinking about structures of unity. We hear at present such expressions as 'covenanting', 'conciliarity', 'the concordat model', 'the uniate model', 'a typology of churches', 'a communion of communions' and so on. What all of these have in common is the recognition that the structures of unity must be such as to maintain in identifiable continuity with their past the several traditions that are to be brought together, so that there will neither be absorption of one group by another nor the levelling down of all in some new hybrid synthetic body. These newer ways of thinking about unity contrast with the older ideal of what was called 'organic union'. Admittedly, this was an ambiguous expression, but its essential flaw was its implicit model or analogy. That analogy comes from biology, with the Church understood as an organism. That analogy has only a limited applicability, and alongside it one has to set analogies of a more personal kind. The prayer of the Fourth Gospel 'that they may all be one' (John 17. 21) did not, of course, envisage the modern problem of unity among the churches, but it is so often quoted that it is well to remember that its model was a personal rather than a biological one, nothing less than the relation of the Father and the Son. In later trinitarian language, this is a relation in which one must neither divide the unity of being nor confound the distinction of persons. This kind of language introduces a type of relationship much more complex than the organic one but far more appropriate when we are considering persons. Unfortunately, as John Macmurray has pointed out,[4] there has been a tendency in the West to reduce the personal to the subpersonal and to think of persons on the analogy of either material things or biological organisms. But persons and groups of persons deserve to be understood in categories no less than personal.

This understanding of the uniqueness of the personal has been well expounded by the present Holy Father in his philosophical treatise, *The Acting Person*.[5] There he advocates 'the principle of dialogue' as 'very aptly suited to the structure of human communities'. He tells us that 'the principle of dialogue allows us to select and bring to light what in controversial situations is right and true; dialogue, in fact, without evading the strains, the conflicts or the strife manifest in the life of various human communities takes up what is right and true in these differences, what may become a source of good for men.'[6] Though the Pope was writing of human communities in general, his remarks have an obvious application to the ecumenical question and acknowledge that whatever was right and valuable in our different traditions deserves to be treated with respect. Unity on the personal level (and this is the richest unity of all) acknowledges and enhances the distinctness of the persons, and certainly can never be achieved by absorption or by the mere abolition of difference.

The need for difference within the unity of any great Church of the future arises not only from considerations about the nature of human communities, but also from the fact that the truth of God in Jesus Christ is never fully grasped from any one point of view. Discussing some of the differences between Lutherans and Reformed, Karl Barth has this to say: 'There must be Lutherans and Reformed: not in the shadow of a unitary theology, but as a twofold theological school – for the sake of the truth about the reality of Jesus Christ, which does not admit of being grasped or conceived by any unitary theology, which will always be the object of all theology, and so perhaps inevitably of a twofold theology.'[7] In that last sentence, however, I would want to substitute 'manifold' for 'twofold'.

Before attempting to apply these general principles to the specific question of how Anglicans and Roman Catholics can come to unity, let me say something about Anglicanism and its peculiar contribution, as I see it. Incidentally, I cannot agree with those churchmen who from time to time tell us that they envisage Anglicanism as eventually disappearing into either one worldwide Church or a series of national united churches. That would be absorption, not unity. In a unity envisaged as a community of persons rather than a merging of institutions, the Anglican voice and the Anglican identity will continue to make an enriching contribution to the whole. I would visualize, for instance, a continuing role for the Archbishop of Canterbury not just as diocesan or even as primate, but as spokesman and representative of that strand of Christianity which looks back to St Augustine and has in the succeeding centuries become a worldwide communion with distinctive characteristics.

The ideal of a comprehensive Church, a single communion with a recognizable unity which nevertheless contains within itself a wide variety of theologies and liturgical practices is already in a remarkable degree realized in the Anglican Communion. It comprises more than twenty-five autonomous churches or provinces scattered across the globe, each free to order its affairs, yet all bound together in a remarkable fellowship that rests on a common tradition, communion with the see of Canterbury and participation in various consultative bodies of which the chief is the ten-yearly Lambeth Conference. Many different races and many different forms of Christian life are contained within it, yet it needs no strong central authority to hold it together. The diversity of the communion as a whole is reflected in most of the constituent churches. Anglo-Catholics, conservative Evangelicals and quite far out Liberals have learned to live together within these churches. Admittedly, there have been times of bitter party strife, but there is not much of it today. The different groups have learned to respect each other and to recognize, even if somewhat grudgingly, that each makes a contribution to the life of the whole. Just as the whole communion has no strong central authority, each constituent church allows maximum freedom. If, for instance, a theologian teaches some rather heterodox doctrine, he is not suppressed, and rightly so, for that would not settle the theological question. The issue that he has raised can only be settled by theological discussion. I believe myself that the Anglican Communion exhibits the kind of pluralism which is the mark of a mature, adult society, and yet that pluralism has not degenerated into sheer chaos but is contained within a framework which is impeccably Catholic and has been consciously maintained in continuity with the Church of the early centuries.

In the preceding paragraph, I have deliberately stressed
the virtues of Anglicanism, but critics might say that I have
idealized the picture. To many of them, it seems that
Anglicanism is neither one thing nor another but a tissue of
compromises in which anything goes. Shortly after the
publication of *The Myth of God Incarnate*, a collection of essays
by Anglicans and others questioning the doctrine of the
incarnation, I was sharing a platform with a Roman
Catholic bishop prominent in the ecumenical movement,
and he asked me, ' What do you Anglicans really believe?'. I
tried to explain that one has to distinguish between the
corporate beliefs of the Church and the opinions of
individuals within it. Indeed, this would now be the case in
the Roman communion too, but there the dissidents would
be called to account. But are there even corporate beliefs in
Anglicanism? I think that Stephen Sykes' timely and
thoughtful book, *The Integrity of Anglicanism*, has made it clear
that there is an Anglican position, founded on the Bible, the
creeds, the councils, the theology of the Fathers, all as
interpreted in the Book of Common Prayer or in the family
of prayer books developed from it. 'The present Anglican
church', he writes, 'has incorporated a regulated doctrinal
structure in the content of its liturgy and in the rules
governing its public performance.'[8] Of course, this is not
rigidly laid down in propositional form. We have nothing in
Anglicanism comparable to Denzinger. Yet it is certainly
not a free-for-all. Anglicans affirm the basic doctrines of
Catholic faith, but allow latitude in the interpretation of
these doctrines and believe that free but responsible
theological discussion rather than appeal to a detailed
magisterium is the best way of sifting truth from falsity. This
freedom is one of the things that Anglicans would wish to
carry with them into any wider unity. They would insist
upon it in any arrangements with the Roman Catholic
Church, just as on the other side they have insisted on
Catholic order in discussions with Protestants.

But while the 'Anglican position', as I have called it, can be constructed from the Book of Common Prayer, the Canon Law and important pronouncements of the Lambeth Conference (such as the Lambeth Quadrilateral – properly the Chicago-Lambeth Quadrilateral) or of the Archbishops (such as the Encyclical Letter of 1897 defending Anglican orders), the meaning of the word 'Anglicanism' cannot be fully spelt out in words and sentences. It is also an *ethos*, a way of seeing things and dealing with them which those who belong within the Anglican Communion know and value but which they would find very hard to put into words. It is a good example of what the philosopher Michael Polanyi calls 'tacit knowledge'[9] which one picks up from those who already have it, as an apprentice learns his trade from a journeyman.

How then is this strange phenomenon, the Anglican Communion, so puzzling to outsiders and yet so beloved by those who belong to it, to advance into unity with the Roman Catholic Church? The very diversity of Anglicanism means that some constraints operate from the beginning. Reginald Fuller, who has had much experience representing Anglicans in ecumenical dialogue, says: 'The genuine Anglican ecumenist always looks three ways; to Rome, to Eastern Orthodoxy and to Protestantism.'[10] Of course, looking three ways at once is a difficult exercise, and, as Fuller acknowledges, it may result in never getting anywhere. 'It means', he says, 'that while we desire unity in all three directions, we must never take a step in one direction that would take us further away from either of the other two.' I think this situation is not always understood by Anglicanism's partners in dialogue. There are some Anglicans who would go to great lengths for the sake of reconciliation with Rome, but there are others who are chiefly interested in reconciliation with Protestantism. Is it possible to satisfy both groups without tearing the Anglican Communion apart and destroying that very comprehensiveness which would have to be a feature of any unified Church of the future? I wonder, however, whether the

time has come for Anglicans to take the dialogue with Rome
with the utmost seriousness, and to accord it a measure of
priority over the others. Otherwise, we may be stuck in
dead centre and even at last drop dead there, like Buridan's
ass. Even a generation ago, the various Protestant denominations seemed to be the most natural partners for dialogue,
but several decades of conversations have produced meagre
results. The entry of Rome into active ecumenical endeavour
in the years after Vatican II has inaugurated a new
situation. Rome must in the long run be the centre of unity
and there can be no truly ecumenical concept of unity that
does not include communion with the see of St Peter. The
American New Testament scholar, John Knox, has written
that the 'new openness on the part of Rome is the major,
the miraculous, the incomparably significant ecumenical
fact of our time.'[11] This fact has shifted the centre of gravity
in ecumenical discussions completely. Are Anglicans,
irrespective of churchmanship, prepared to give to the
Anglican–Roman Catholic dialogue a measure of priority
and really go all out for reconciliation, without, of course, as
I have insisted, surrendering whatever is of value in their
own tradition? As Rome has officially recognized in the
Decree on Ecumenism in the Documents of Vatican II, the
Anglican Communion has a special position among the
reformed churches of the West because of its preservation
of 'Catholic traditions and institutions'.[12] How we respond
to Roman overtures may influence many others. If the split
between Rome and Canterbury could be healed, then many
other divisions that have proved stubborn up till now
would soon be overcome.

But how does one go about the reconciliation of Rome
and Canterbury? Much has been done already, and I think it
has been done in the right way. That is to say, it has been a
step-by-step approach. Human beings and their institutions
are historical, they need time to change direction and develop
new ways of thinking and action, and as far as the churches
are concerned, this means that they need to grow together.

121

The first step in the process of growing together has already met with a success that has gone far beyond expectations – I mean, setting forth the measure of agreement that already obtains between the two communions. I have in mind chiefly the splendid achievement of ARCIC, expressed in the three Agreed Statements. I shall say more about them in a moment. Here I simply want to say that the official activities of ARCIC have gone on against the background of widespread contacts that have led the rank and file (both clerical and lay) of both communions to discover that in spite of four hundred years of separate existence, to say nothing of much hostility, they are still so close to each other in doctrine, liturgy and polity. Even if the church authorities on both sides still take a long time to advance toward a fuller degree of unity, the old separateness has been brought to an end. Just to give one example, when I began teaching theology about thirty years ago, I do not believe I had met any Roman Catholic theologians, I had read very few of their books, and I had no Roman Catholic students. Now the interchange at the theological level is very brisk indeed, and the full effects of this will become apparent in the future.

But let me come back to the Agreed Statements. These, as I have said, constitute the obvious first step toward unity, for they set up the framework within which a communion of communions can be established. They do not reveal complete identity of view on the matters which have been considered, but they do bring to light basic parameters within which different interpretations may be permissible.

It must be said, however, that the three statements are of unequal value. Obviously, the two communions were already in substantial agreement about the central doctrines of the Christian faith, and it was a bold step to select for discussion the three controversial questions of the Eucharist, the ordained ministry and authority. The statements show that the problems are not intractable, but with varying degrees of success in each case.

The statement on the Eucharist appears to me the weakest of the three, though it could have been much stronger. Of course, this was the first of these exercises, and it was to be hoped that they would improve with practice. One obvious fault of the Windsor statement was simply its extreme brevity – four short pages. A statement of this kind is, admittedly, not meant to be a theological treatise, but greater depth of treatment was needed. But a more serious problem concerns the methodology behind the statement. It might have been wise if ARCIC, before issuing any statement on a substantive theological issue, had explored what measure of agreement there is between the two communions on the doing of theology. Neither Rome nor Canterbury stands for a strictly biblicist theology – both indeed seek the foundations of doctrine in the Bible but, unlike some Protestant denominations, they acknowledge also the place of tradition and the legitimate development of doctrine from its New Testament origins. But for some reason ARCIC was very biblicist in its treatment of the Eucharist. Thus the difficult notions of eucharistic sacrifice and eucharistic presence were made to rest very largely on a highly dynamic exegesis of the Greek word *anamnesis*, 'memorial'. The exegesis may be correct, but there are scholars who contest it,[13] and *by itself* it provides an insecure basis for what ARCIC wanted to say. Even more questionable is the later statement that, 'The Lord's words at the last supper, "Take and eat; this is my body", do not allow us to dissociate the gift of the presence and the act of sacramental eating.' The purpose of this statement is obscure (because of the brevity of the document) but the point I want to make is that the commands to eat and drink are contained only in St Matthew's account of the institution, and it is virtually certain that they were not part of the Lord's original words.[14] In this case we do not have even a probable exegesis and the attempt to be strictly biblical fails again. Here it may not matter very much, since it is so unclear

123

what ARCIC was trying to establish by the quotation. To some extent, these two points, especially the first of them, have been clarified in ARCIC's official 'Elucidations' of the statement, and the biblical teaching on the Eucharist has been supplemented by an appeal to patristic and later theology.

Very much better is the statement on ministry and ordination. It is more than twice as long as the statement on the Eucharist and so is able to treat the questions more adequately. What is more important, it does not try to derive a doctrine of ministry *solely* from the New Testament, but implicitly recognizes the legitimacy of subsequent development in such matters as the threefold ministry of bishops, presbyters and deacons, and the use of priestly language about the ordained Christian ministry. The thinking here was in fact very close to that of the Lambeth Conference of 1930, which declared:

> The episcopate occupies a position which is, in point of historical development, analogous to that of the canon of scripture and the creeds. In the first days, there was no canon of the New Testament scripture, for the books afterward included in it were still being written. The canon was slowly formed and the acceptance of a single canon throughout the Church took several generations. So, too, the Apostles' Creed is the result of a process of growth which we can in large measure trace. If the episcopate, as we find it universally by the end of the second century, was the result of a like process of adaptation and growth, that would be no evidence that it lacked divine authority, but rather that the life of the Spirit within the Church had found it to be the most appropriate organ for the functions it discharged.[15]

Commenting on the above, Reginald Fuller writes: 'We can only justify our institutions in terms of legitimate development. This applies to priesthood, episcopacy and succession. Could it also, for Anglicans, legitimate the development of the primacy of the Bishop of Rome?'[16] Here we have another direct question to Anglicans, and one that leads us to the third of the Agreed Statements. This document has been perhaps less well received than the other two and has been rather severely criticized by some prominent Anglicans. Nevertheless, it does seem to me to have opened ways forward on what is likely to prove the most difficult problem of all – that of the papacy in a unified Church. Both Anglicans and Roman Catholics already have bishops or archbishops who have a certain primacy within a province or country. This is not an autocratic power, but is closely associated with such ideas as collegiality and conciliarity. On the other hand, it is not a mere primacy of honour. A primate is not a mere figurehead, but a leader and inspirer. Since the principle of primacy is already accepted by Anglicans, should it not be possible for them to find ways toward recognizing the universal primacy of the Bishop of Rome and so restoring communion with that see? We are told by ARCIC that this would not imply submission to an authority that would stifle the distinctive features of the local churches. It is in this connection that we might consider the continuing role of the Archbishop of Canterbury which I mentioned earlier – and with him, of course, the other Anglican primates. Could the papal primacy be mediated to the Anglican Communion through its existing primates, and, presumably, exercised in the manner in which Anglicans have come to understand primacy? For this to happen, there would need to be established a true collegiality between the Pope and the Anglican primates with regular meetings as a council.

I have not faced the question of infallibility. I once wrote that it seemed to me that papal infallibility is an insuperable obstacle between Roman Catholics and Anglicans, but I no longer think so. I changed my mind on reading some explanatory comments by Bishop B. C. Butler. In the first instance, he wrote that 'infallibility' is an unfortunate term, for it seems to express the negative idea of inerrancy, whereas it is meant to have the positive significance that when the mind of the Church is open to the Holy Spirit, then it will be led into truth. In the second place, he made it clear that such truth does not attach to particular verbal formulations, which are always infected by historical or cultural relativity, but to what he called the 'governing intention' expressed in the formulations.[17] There is not space here to develop these ideas, but they are clearly promising, and it is likely that further discussion and, we may hope, eventual convergence will take place along these lines. Incidentally, Hans Küng's attempt to identify infallibility with the indefectibility of the Church is not, in my opinion, helpful, for it rests on a confusion. 'Indefectibility' is an eschatological idea, but when we talk of 'infallibility', we are asking about the kind of guidance available to the Church *in via*.

I have put two straight questions to Anglicans. Now it is time to put one to Roman Catholics. Are these three Agreed Statements, together with all the background of tacit agreement behind them, enough for us to take the next step toward unity? That next step would, I think, be full intercommunion between our two communions, and I would hope that this would also carry with it recognition of one another's ordained ministries, with the possibility, properly regulated, of priests of the one communion serving when required in the other. This bald statement about intercommunion and interchangeability of ministries would need, of course, to be spelt out in detailed ways. Presumably some service of reconciliation would be needed to heal the breach of centuries and to express in appropriate liturgical and theological ways the new relationship. Just what these ways might be needs thought, for there is no precedent for such a step, but surely a way can be found which safeguards what each communion values in its tradition, a way to unity without absorption. I would think too that any establishment of intercommunion would need not just to be inaugurated but would also require continuing arrangements for the maintenance of a living fellowship. I have mentioned already the possibility of a council of primates to relate the two communions at the highest level, but in every region there should be councils of bishops for the development of true collegiality and the formation of agreed strategies of mission and service.

What further steps toward unity might be taken beyond what is proposed here, I do not think we need to ask. That can be left to a future generation. The 'step-by-step' approach will leave us with some untidiness, but I think it is only by growing together that human beings and human institutions can form new relations. I have always been highly suspicious of any cut and dried schemes of union that set a date and suppose that on that date unity has been achieved. Among the untidinesses that would arise in a step-by-step approach would be the existence side by side in many parts of the world of parallel episcopates, the duplication of administrative machinery (for the councils I visualize would be consultative), the overlapping of pastoral care and so on. There would be other loose ends – for instance, where some branches of the Anglican Communion have ordained women to the priesthood, it could not be expected that they would be permitted to officiate in Roman Catholic churches, just as at present they are not permitted to officiate in the Church of England. But these differences of discipline and practice between one province of the church and another have not been allowed to break communion among the Anglican churches, and I do not see that it should prevent communion between the Anglican churches and the Roman Catholic Church.

It would be idle to deny that even the steps described here cannot be taken without a great deal of thought and discussion, and without some pain on both sides. But given goodwill, it should not be impossible. If both Anglicans and Roman Catholics can return a firm and sincere 'Yes!' to the questions posed earlier in this essay, then I think they will find themselves moving almost naturally into deeper relations with each other. Or is that just a dream? The very fact that things have changed so much in the past twenty years or so and that there has been such a miraculous growth in understanding is surely sufficient proof that it need not be just a dream. On the other hand, if we delay too long in going on to the next step, then it may all fade away, and we shall have to say that after all, it was just a dream.

NOTES

1 L. Kolakowski, *Main Currents of Marxism* (Clarendon Press 1978), I, p. 3.

2 K. Rahner, *The Christian of the Future* (New York 1967), p. 34.

3 ibid., p. 32.

4 J. Macmurray, *The Self as Agent* (Faber & Faber 1967), pp. 33ff.

5 Karol Wojtyla (Pope John Paul II), *The Acting Person* (Dordrecht 1979), p. 287.

6 ibid.

7 K. Barth, *Church Dogmatics*, I/2, (T. & T. Clark 1956), p. 171.

8 Stephen Sykes, *The Integrity of Anglicanism* (Mowbray 1978), p. 47.

9 M. Polanyi, *Personal Knowledge* (New York 1964), pp. 49ff.

10 R. H. Fuller, 'The Anglican Ecumenical Stance' in *Realistic Reflections on Church Union*, ed. J. Macquarrie (Albany, NY, 1967), p. 11.

11 John Knox, 'A Plea for a Wider Ecumenism', ibid., p. 28.

12 *The Documents of Vatican II*, ed. Walter M. Abbott SJ (Geoffrey Chapman, London-Dublin, 1966), p. 356.

13 See, e.g., P. E. Hughes, 'Eucharistic Agreement?' in *A Critique of Eucharistic Agreement*, ed. J. Lawrence (SPCK 1975), p. 58.

14 J. Jeremias, *The Eucharistic Words of Jesus* (New York 1966), p. 165.

15 *The Lambeth Conference 1930* (SPCK 1930), p. 130.

16 R. H. Fuller, 'The Ministry in the New Testament', in *Episcopalians and Roman Catholics: Can They Ever Get Together?*, ed. H. J. Ryan and J. R. Wright (Denville, NJ, 1972), p. 103.

17 B. C. Butler, 'Roman Requirements' in *The Tablet*, 5 July 1975, p. 624.

7

Corporate Union and the Body Politic

Constitutional aspects of union between
the Church of England and the Church of Rome

G. R. Dunstan

1

'A two-headed organ is a dreadful monster': *organum anceps monstrum horrendum.* Canonists[1] will recognize the words, for they are their own. Fashioned as a weapon in the Pope's defence against the medieval Emperor, they were turned against the Pope by national sovereigns in the century after the Conciliar Movement – the attempt to reform the Church by means of General Councils in the early 1400s – and nowhere more effectively than in Tudor England. They established the terms of the question which we discuss still today: what constitutional relation is possible between a canonically governed Church and a sovereign state? The question is complicated when the Church in question, and its government, transcend the frontiers of national sovereignties. But let us begin where we are, with the English Church and nation.

For the Church of England the constitutional relation is formally expressed in the revised Canons finally promulged, with the Royal Licence, in 1969. I select:

A 1   The Church of England, established according to the laws of this realm under the Queen's Majesty, belongs to the

129

true and apostolic Church of Christ; and, as our duty to the said Church of England requires, we do constitute and ordain that no member thereof shall be at liberty to maintain or hold the contrary.

A 5   The doctrine of the Church of England is grounded in the holy Scriptures, and in such teachings of the ancient Fathers and Councils of the Church as are agreeable to the said Scriptures. In particular such doctrine is to be found in the Thirty-nine Articles of Religion, the Book of Common Prayer, and the Ordinal.

A 6   The government of the Church of England under the Queen's Majesty, by archbishops, bishops, deans, provosts, archdeacons, and the rest of the clergy and of the laity that bear office in the same, is not repugnant to the Word of God.

A 7   We acknowledge that the Queen's most excellent Majesty, acting according to the laws of the realm, is the highest power under God in this kingdom, and has supreme authority over all persons in all causes, as well ecclesiastical as civil.

C 13   [Requires an Oath of Allegiance of all persons, being British subjects, before ordination or consecration, election or translation to any bishopric, institution to any benefice or licencing to any perpetual curacy, lectureship or preacher-ship.]

G 1   [Provides for Diocesan and Provincial Courts and Commissions, in accordance with the Ecclesiastical Jurisdiction Measure 1963, and, further, that]
4   There may be appointed by Her Majesty a Commission of Review, to review any finding of the Court of Ecclesiastical Causes Reserved or of any Commission of the Upper House of the Convocations appointed for the trial of a bishop or an archbishop.
[and]
5   Her Majesty in Council has jurisdiction to hear appeals from the Court of Arches or the Chancery Court in faculty causes not involving matter of doctrine, ritual, or cere-monial.

Thus far the canons. Other features of the constitutional position are these (though not all are mentioned):

The duty and prescriptive right of the Archbishop of Canterbury to anoint and crown the Sovereign and to administer the Coronation oath; and of certain other bishops to take traditional parts in the ceremony.

The statutory duty of the Sovereign to maintain 'the protestant reformed religion' and the statutory denial of inheritance or enjoyment of the Crown to anyone who 'is or shall be reconciled to or shall hold communion with the see or Church of Rome or shall profess the popish religion or shall marry a papist' – obstacles set up, not in pious times at the Reformation, but as late as 1685 and 1700.

The requirement of a Royal Licence to convene the Convocations (continued from the Middle Ages) and to enact and promulge canons (imposed at the Reformation).

The session as of right of the two Archbishops and twenty-four senior bishops in the House of Lords.

The formal submission of Acts of the General Synod, via appropriate Committees, for either acceptance *in toto* or rejection by both Houses of Parliament, in order that, as Measures, they may enjoy the same authority as Acts of Parliament or Statutes of the Realm.

The obligation of Cathedral Chapters to seek a Royal Licence to elect a new bishop, and the right of the Sovereign to nominate whom they shall elect – both continued from medieval practice, though modified now by a convention which enables a church committee to suggest two names in preferential order to the Sovereign.

The right of access of all Her Majesty's subjects to the parish church and the pastoral ministrations of the parish priest in whatever place where they dwell, and irrespective of whether they profess 'membership' of the Church of England or of any other Church or religious persuasion or of none; and the duty of the Church of England and its clergy to minister to them.

131

The Royal Prerogative to assure continuity in the cure of souls by presenting to benefices 'by reason of lapse' should the patron, diocesan bishop and archbishop in turn fail to do so in due time; seldom exercised now, however, in view of the widespread suspension of presentation by bishops in the stated interest of 'pastoral re-organization'.

The financial provision by Parliament for Chaplains to the Speaker of the House of Commons, to H. M. Prisons and the Armed Forces; and the appointment by Lord High Sheriffs of their honorary chaplains, who attend H. M. Judges of Assize.

The maintenance by Her Majesty of an Ecclesiastical Household, consisting of a Chapel Royal, an episcopal Almoner and episcopal Clerk to the Closet, Chaplains, Priests and clerks.

That is an outline of the constitutional picture. Few features of it, in fact, stem directly from the Tudor embrace of the canonical dictum with which I began, *organum anceps monstrum horrendum*; for the English are a pragmatic race, on the whole, not given overmuch to contriving institutions in obedience to theories. Most of it has been shaped by history, a history begun in Anglo-Saxon England. And it was by an appeal to that history, those historic origins, that King Henry VIII, in the preambles to his earliest Reformation statutes, justified his repudiation of dual headship, a sovereignty divided between himself and the Pope, and declared the English monarch to be in all causes, ecclesiastical as well as civil, supreme.

2

We misunderstand the English Reformation if we read it primarily as either a theological or a political event. It was in origin a conflict between lawyers, common lawyers and canonists, a major eruption after centuries of tension between them. Political opportunism, exercised by the King through the instrumentality of Parliament, gave a qualified victory to common lawyers in the Inns of Court; Doctors' Commons, the home of the civilians and canonists, survived for three more centuries, until defeated by its own decay. (Theology was an after-thought.) The conflict is best studied in the writings of Christopher St German, a godly common lawyer of the Middle Temple, particularly in his *Doctor and Student*, a Dialogue between a Doctor of Divinity and a Student in the Laws of England, published in Latin in 1523, in English in 1531, and many times reprinted. His work had, I believe, an influence on the drafting of the Henrician statutes awaiting scholarly research; timing, substance and literary parallels suggest it.

His problem, and ours, was the coexistence of two jurisdictions within one realm, dating from the Norman introduction into England of the reforms imposed by Pope Gregory VII to 'free' the Church from lay control: the common law courts, in which the royal judges administered customary and statute law, and by procedures related to the concept of 'liberties'; and the spiritual or ecclesiastical courts, in which ecclesiastical judges administered the canon law, and by procedures developed out of the civil law of Rome. Both procedures relied heavily upon the oath; but in the common law the accused could not be made to incriminate himself, whereas in the civil and canon law he could. Appeal in the royal courts was to the King; in the ecclesiastical courts, to the Pope. Two jurisdictions in one realm.

St German's method was to set out cases of conscience in which those subject to these laws, laymen as well as clerks, were torn between their conflicting claims, putting themselves in peril of the temporal courts if, at the behest of the canon law, they offended against custom or statute, and of excommunication and penance in the spiritual courts if, in obedience to custom or statute, they defied the canon. Instances were plentiful, invading lay and economic life as well as clerical and ecclesiastical. Patronage and the right of presentation to benefices, the liability of abbots in law without their chapters, the legitimation of children by subsequent marriage, the 'providing' by the Pope of incumbents to benefices and high ecclesiastical dignities, the paying or witholding of tithes from felled timber, alienation of land from secular use to the Church in perpetuity, clerical privilege or 'benefit of clergy' to immunity from sentence in the royal courts on criminal charges – and more also. In short,

> it is troublous to the people to have two powers within the realm, whereby they may be sued of one thing in several courts, and by several authorities.[2]

Canon law, he said, embodied in part the law of God, natural and revealed, in part the law of the Church. In tithe-paying, for example, the obligation of temporal men to give to the support of spiritual men is a law of God; the obligation to give an arithmetical tenth is a law of the Church: it was therefore mutable and admitted as a custom in this realm only by sufferance of the temporal power, and so open to regulation by the temporal power. By openly defying the custom of the realm as in the case of *Sylva Caedua*, that is the tithing of timber wood (forbidden by the Statute of Carlisle), the canonists

> set law against custom, power against power, and in a manner the spiritualty against the temporalty, whereby they might know that great variance and suit would follow . . . They did not follow the direct order of charity therein so perfectly as they might have done.

They have merely threatened and excommunicated those who obeyed the law of the realm and have done nothing to ease conscience of its burdens. He would have the great fifteenth-century textbook of canon law, still authoritative then, Lyndwode's *Provinciale*, purged of those constitutions, both of provincial synods and those promulgated by papal legates, which are against the king's law and prerogative, so that young men studying the canons should no longer be deceived by them.

He allows to the Pope and the spiritual men their authority to determine spiritual principles; but where those principles are to be embodied in customs, and so touch the King's subjects and his lands, there Parliament has a competence to regulate, to change and to abolish. Since a schism in the papacy threatens the realm with schism, King and Parliament have power to determine which claimant shall be accounted Pope within the realm. Parliament had often legislated in the past on church affairs, so helping the bishops to implement their canons (which was true), and should do so now, because the Ordinaries were more concerned to punish than to provide relief. But since Parliament should proceed, not by way of imposition but with consent, he would have study begun now, with spiritual men and temporal men 'charitably laying their heades together' to instruct the Parliament 'when the need shall require'. Together they should charitably decide

> what they think be immediately grounded upon the law of God, or upon the law of reason, or what not. For commonly the parliament hath over these laws no direct power, but to strengthen them, and to make them to be more surely kept it hath power.

In *The Power of the Clergy and the Laws of the Realm*, written soon after the Act of Supremacy, 1534, he wrote of that Act

> that the kynges grace hathe no newe auctorite by that he is confessed by the clergy and auctorysed by the parlyment to be head of the churche of Englande. For it is only a declaracyon of his fyrst power comytted to the kynglye and regall auctorite and no new graunte. And that for all the power that he is the heed of the churche, that yet hath none auctorite to minister any of the sacraments ne to do any other thying spirituall, wherof oure lorde gave power only to his apostles and discyples . . . It is no dout but that such power as the clergy hath by the immediate graunte of Christ the kyng ne in his parlyment can nat take it from theym, thoughe they maye order the manner of the doynge.

This position he justifies from Scripture, taking the proof texts one by one. On'show it unto the Church', which some took to mean 'show it to the clergy' he writes

> To that it may be answered that by that worde chyrche is nat understande only the clergye, for they undoubtedly make nat the chyrche, for the hole congregation of Christen people maketh the chyrch.

It seemed to me worthwhile to take this route into our question, because it stems from a genuine dialogue with the canon lawyers upon the constitutional place of the Church in the realm, and because it was both instrumental and expressive of the immediate changes which provided for the continuing Church of England its present constitutional place. The legal Reformation followed very closely the course which St German indicated for it – including plans for a commision of thirty-two, half of temporal men, half of spiritual, to reform the canon law, plans which recurred over the next hundred years, but which were never fulfilled. The Henrician statutes, by restraining appeals to Rome, and by converting the canon law into the King's ecclesiastical law, restored a unified jurisdiction to the realm: the Sovereign became the fount of *justice*, in causes spiritual as well as temporal. The ecclesiastical courts became one of a series of courts, varying in their procedures, exercising jurisdiction from the Crown: that is the strict meaning of the Royal *Supremacy*, for which the Anglo-French word is Sovereignty. The statutes were repealed under Mary, though she continued to exercise powers resting on the equivalent medieval statutes, as when she ordered the seizure of papal bulls directed against Reginald Pole, Cardinal Archbishop of Canterbury; the statutes were restored, with modification, by Elizabeth I. Elizabeth took the title Supreme Governor of the Church of England, instead of Supreme Head; in substance there was no change, though in concept there was; and Elizabeth used her power consistently to protect the Church from the meddling of Parliament.

In the light of this historical sketch, incidentally, it is highly significant that in the Final Statement of ARCIC concerning a possible new relation between the Church of England and the Roman Catholic Church, the position envisaged for the Bishop of Rome is one of *Primacy*, that is, of being first among equals, not one of *Supremacy*, that is, of Sovereignty over the uniting Churches (*Authority in the Church II*, paras. 16–22).

3

I emphasized earlier the historical and pragmatic origins of this process. It was not, however, without theoretical justification; and this was given lapidary expression, before the close of the sixteenth century, by Richard Hooker in his fundamental treatise, *Of the Laws of Ecclesiastical Polity*.[3]

Hooker contended that Catholic and Puritan alike drove a false division between Church and commonwealth, maintaining as they did that 'the walls of separation between these two must for ever be upheld'. Their error was to treat exceptional circumstances, like the exile of the Jews in Egypt or in Babylon, or the early Church under persecution, as normative. On the contrary,

With us . . .the name of a church importeth only a society of men, first united into some public form of regiment, and secondly distinguished from other societies by the exercise of Christian religion . . .

We hold, that seeing there is not any man of the Church of England but the same man is also a member of the commonwealth; nor any man a member of the commonwealth, which is not also of the Church of England; therefore as in a figure triangular the base doth differ from the sides thereof, and yet one and the self-same line is both a base and also a side; a side simply, a base if it chance to be the bottom and underlie the rest; so, albeit properties and actions of one kind do cause the name of commonwealth, qualities and functions of another sort the name of a Church to be given unto a multitude, yet one and the selfsame multitude may in such sort be both, and is so with us, that no person appertaining to the one can be denied to be also of the other (VIII. i. 2).

Hence it is proper that bishops should occupy themselves with the affairs of the commonwealth, and that kings should make laws for the Church. This - and Stephen Gardiner, Bishop of Winchester under the old régime, and a Doctor of Civil and of Canon Law of the University of Cambridge, had written to the same effect in *De vera obedientia* in 1535 - this is at the heart of the theory of establishment: it underlies the claim of every subject of the realm to the pastoral care of his parish priest, and the duty of the parish priest so to care for every soul within his parish. The Church is an efficacious sign (*sacramentum*) within and to the nation of the reality of grace.

Olivier Loyer, at the end of his profound and illuminating exposition of Hooker on this theme, asks questions pertinent today, when, on the one hand, the identity of Church and commonwealth is visibly repudiated, and, on the other, 'union' of some sort is in contemplation between the Church of England as by Law Established and the Roman Catholic Church with its own jurisdiction stemming from Rome and transcending all national frontiers.

> Est-il vraiment possible d'avoir une unité sociale sans une unité juridictionnelle et une unité juridictionnelle sans unité de gouvernement? On bute toujours sur la même difficulté: dans une chrétienté brisée, divisée en corps chrétiens indépendants et souverains, peut-on conserver l'unité sociale et politique de l'Église visible universelle, si l'on refuse de la considérer elle-même comme un corps autonome et parfait? (op. cit., II. 586)*

Hooker himself had no difficulty in reconciling his concept of a national Church with the universality of that One, Holy, Catholic and Apostolic Church of which he

* Is it possible to have a unity of fellowship without juridical unity, and a juridical unity without unity of government? Always we come up against the same difficulty: in a fragmented Christianity, broken up into independent and sovereign Christian bodies, how is it possible to preserve the unity in fellowship and polity of the universal Church visable while refusing to regard that Church as one autonomous and perfect body?

knew the Church of England to be part. We recall the famous figure of the sea:

> By the Church therefore in this question we understand no other than only the visible Church. For preservation of Christianity there is not anything more needful, than that such as are of the visible Church have mutual fellowship and society one with another. In which consideration, as the main body of the sea being one, yet within divers precincts hath divers names; so the Catholic Church is in like sort divided into a number of distinct Societies, every of which is termed a Church within itself. In this sense the Church is always a visible society of men; not an assembly but a society . . . As therefore they that are of the mystical body of Christ have those inward graces and virtues, whereby they differ from all others, which are not of the same body; again whosoever appertain to the visible body of the Church, they have also the notes of external profession, whereby the world knoweth what they are: after the same manner even the several societies of Christian men, unto every of which the name of a Church is given with addition betokening severalty, as the Church of Rome, Corinth, Ephesus, England, and so the rest, must be endued with correspondent general properties belonging unto them as they are public Christian societies. And of such properties common to all societies Christian, it may not be denied that one of the very chiefest is Ecclesiastical Polity (III. i. 14).

Christ, having universal dominion, is the fount of order, and of authority to preach the word, to administer the sacraments, and so to define the faith which is derived from the one and which enfolds the other. This authority he has committed inalienably to his Church – the temporal power may not intermeddle with it. Episcopal government, as an evidenced derivation from apostolic oversight, is a proper part of that order – though Hooker would not unchurch those churches which, in his own time, for historical reasons, were deprived of it. The unity of the Church, therefore, as a matter of faith, order and spiritual or sacramental communion, was no problem to him in principle – given the necessary controversies about truth and error, purity and impurity and so on which are inherent in the Church's life. But that union did not imply concentrating

139

supremacy in one central jurisdiction, and it could not. Christ, having universal dominion, was the source of jurisdiction, the fount of law and justice also; and this he entrusted, as we have seen, to distinct societies, sovereign nations, in which Church and commonwealth were one. On this ground stands the Church of England's acknowledgement of the Royal Supremacy. Is it tolerable to the canonical mind of the Roman Catholic Church?

4

It is time to ask how, granted other developments and changes, in a restored communion, or union in some form, between the Church of Rome and the Church of England, church and nation could conceivably accommodate themselves in a constitutional relationship.

First the concept of establishment itself must be faced. It is everywhere, ecclesiastically speaking, out of fashion. The Second Vatican Council, in *Gaudium et Spes*, S. 76, asserted that 'the Church is quite distinct from the political community and uncommitted to any political system'; 'the political community and the Church in their respective fields are independent and autonomous'. (It went on to commend reasonable co-operation.) The assertion was embodied in the draft of the *Lex Ecclesiae Fundamentalis* (the proposed Fundamental Law to accompany the revised Code of Canon Law), in canon 86 of the Schema of 1971. I do not recall what happened to the canon in subsequent drafts, but it is unlikely to have been amended. Forgotten are the words of Disraeli's Cardinal Grandison, that the separation of Church and state, evidenced by the lamented absence of Princes from the coming first Vatican Council, meant that 'society is no longer consecrated'; but not forgotten is the attempted de-consecration of the Church by the state in the embraces of Mussolini and Adolf Hitler. In Britain, the Irish and Welsh provinces of the old United Church of England and Ireland have been disestablished, for historical reasons conditioned largely by nationalistic sentiment. It is easy to provoke calls for disestablishment in the Church of England whenever what earnest clergymen see as 'spiritual liberties' appear to be threatened; yet whenever formal Commissions are appointed to examine the matter, invariably they advise some modification of the establishment rather than its dissolution. There has been no serious attempt by the state so far to disestablish the Church of England by means of a Bill in Parliament, or even a Green Paper or White Paper preparatory to one. The Church of Scotland, Presbyterian in constitution, remains established – the Queen becomes a Presbyterian in her Scottish domain – and its form was for long coveted as a model by some libertarians in England.

What, first, of the principle of establishment itself – that the state should formally profess its submission to the sovereignty of God and his redemption wrought in Christ, and that the Church should publicly profess its responsibility for ministering that redemption to every person in the land? Despite appearances, and assertions to the contrary, there is a sense in which Hooker's belief in a unity between Church and commonwealth is still tenable. If, as we believe, baptism confers a real unity in the Body of Christ, and if a common citizenship implies a unity in the body politic, there must thereby be constituted, in the persons of the baptized, a unity of these two bodies, despite denominational schism in the Church and social fragmentation in the commonwealth. Establishment gives this unity institutional embodiment. *Gaudium et Spes*, S. 40, comes near to this concept of the Church as the ensoulment of human society, though in more diffuse language, and without institutional establishment.

At present in England one church only is established, the Church of England; the others are not. There are precedents for modification. In the Swiss cantons there are *églises reconnues*: 'establishment', to the extent of recognition and the collection of church taxes, extends to Catholic, Old

Catholic, Reformed and Protestant Churches according to local tradition, perhaps three or four in the same canton. Informally England has moved already in this direction. On major national ecclesiastical occasions, including the Coronation, places are made for participation by dignitaries of other Churches alongside those to whom the constitution assigns a part. The Cardinal Archbishop of Westminster is quoted on moral or social issues in parallel with the Archbishop of Canterbury; so is the Chief Rabbi; and speakers from the so-called Free Churches, and the British Council of Churches, are assumed to be heard with authority in the name of 'religion'. At least one distinguished Nonconformist minister has been created a Life Peer, to complement the establishment of Prelates in the House of Lords. Establishment, then, need not be exclusive; there are buds already formed from which new limbs of a new body corporate might grow.

Within the establishment, what of the place of the Sovereign? Traditionally in Christian thought he has been a *mixta persona*, vested in hieratic coronation robes, and invested as such with supremacy, sovereignty, as the fount of justice and mercy in the land. So Hooker writes:

> A gross error it is, to think that regal power ought to serve for the good of the body, and not of the soul; for men's temporal peace, and not for their eternal safety; as if God had ordained kings for no other end and purpose but only to fat up men like hogs, and to see that they have their mast (VIII. iii. 2).

The crude anti-Catholic provisions of the statutes of 1685 and 1700 would require modification: what Parliament has enacted Parliament can repeal. A Bill for the repeal would, no doubt, provoke a duet from Mr Paisley and Mr Powell, with a supporting chorus of protest from Northern Ireland; and the concurrence of Commonwealth legislatures would be required; but neither difficulty is insuperable.

The royal licence to convene Convocations, a requirement predating the Reformation by two and a half centuries, has not in fact proved inhibiting since the early eighteenth century, when members of both Houses of the Canterbury Convocation were meddling actively in the bed-chamber politics of the time, and were justly restrained. The liberty of the General Synod to authorize liturgical change, for better or for worse, is now established, subject only to Parliamentary insistence that the Book of Common Prayer shall remain available for use and as a doctrinal formulary in the Church of England. The function of Parliament herein is not to dictate forms or content of the Church's worship, but to protect liberties of Her Majesty's subjects which enthusiasm for innovation is liable to assail, and has in fact assailed. Similarly, the function of the ecclesiastical courts is not to formulate the Church's doctrine, but to declare what are legitimate constructions of the Church's formularies – a judicial function made easier, not only by training in the rules of construction, but also by a professional distance from theological or ecclesiastical controversy. And this jurisdiction is appellate: that is, it is exercised only on appeal from litigants who believe themselves to be denied justice in the Church's domestic courts.

The nomination by the Crown of bishops and deans, as of Regius Professors, Poets Laureate and the like, stands on history, the royal prerogative. It was a regular feature of medieval practice. Successors of the founder of a monastery, for instance, retained patron's rights: on the occurrence of a vacancy the chapter sought a licence from the patron to elect a new abbot or prior, and with his *congé* he would send the name of the brother whom he wished the chapter to elect; and once elected the new prelate sought confirmation from the patron. In the appointment or translation of bishops, the royal licence was a factor in the triangle of forces between the cathedral chapter, the papacy and the Crown, sometimes in collusion with the papacy, sometimes in opposition. Its justification lay in the importance of bishops as magnates of the realm, as Lords of Parliament and as holding jurisdiction over extensive spiritual and temporal estates. The feudal accidents have fallen away;

but the point of substance remains. Are bishops and deans still to be men of such stature, and their offices still of such significance, that they count for something in the national life? that it matters who shall occupy these positions? If so, the Crown is the apt embodiment of the national interest. The danger of manipulation for purposes of state is recognized – and evidence of this abuse is not absent from the contemporary world. But the Sovereign can nominate for episcopal election only those whom the Church has ordained priests and is willing to consecrate as bishops. Resistance to tyranny is always possible. Neither is the Church always innocent of intrigue nor always of unerring wisdom in its choices. In short, this exercise of the royal prerogative is as much an exercise of sovereignty, *supremitas*, in the Church of England as the papal nomination of bishops is in the Church of Rome. By modern convention the prerogative is seldom exercised in either church without local consultation.

5

This paper is singular, perhaps idiosyncratic, insofar as its author happens to believe in what he describes. He is not apologetic, as many are, for the establishment – though whether his *apologia* for it carries conviction his readers must judge. His reading of history has not commended the Church to him as distinctive for its concept and custody of justice. On the whole he believes the common law tradition to have proved a more reliable guardian of personal liberty than the canonical. When the royal justice has been appealed to for the declaration of doctrine, as in the trial of Mr Gorham whose understanding of baptismal regeneration his bishop declared unorthodox in the mid-nineteenth century, the judgements have been generally to preserve latitude in the Church's own teaching: refusing to condemn Gorham it refused to tie the Church exclusively to one possible interpretation of its own formularies, so respecting theological liberty. Without venturing any judgement upon the substance of the theological controversies ventilated in the Roman Catholic Church in recent years – concerning Schillebeeckx, say, and Küng – it is apposite to register some disquiet at the process by which the issues appear to be tried. As at the time of Christopher St German, there is a lack of sympathy between two traditions, that of the common law and that of the canonist and civilian; though we may now, perhaps, perceive and discuss them in charity.[4] The scope of the Roman canon law is wider, too, than English churchmen recognize. We are less ready than the Roman Church, in our Anglican tradition, to signal our moral prescriptions, and even our ecclesiastical obligations (at least so far as concerns laymen not exercising ecclesiastical office), in terms of law: we speak of them simply as obligations in conscience. And this difference works its way through, I suspect, into pastoral practice, into what the parish priest (as we call him) or the diocesan priest (as our cousins call him) says to his parishioners from the pulpit and in their homes.

'Spiritual freedom' is, of course, a myth, if by that is meant a total separation of Church and state. Any body corporate holding property holds it on trust for certain purposes and, so far as religious bodies are concerned, in relation to certain stated doctrines. Fidelity in the execution of such trust is cognizable at law, in the Royal Courts of Justice. Members of Churches are also subjects of the Queen, subject to customary and statute law; they have liberties also which the law will protect. The courts are open. Parliament may enact, indeed, has enacted, statutes permitting conduct, relationships or status which the Church would prefer to leave forbidden. Matrimonial causes, for instance, remained the prerogative of the church courts (subject to procedure by private Bill in the High Court of Parliament) until 1855; then they were transferred to the Queen's courts, and Parliament has legislated to convert the old canonical remedies of *divorcium* into the modern law of divorce. The Churches of Britain, while unanimous in upholding, as they must, the first principles of the marriage covenant as confirmed by our Lord in Scripture, vary in their response to secular divorce. Whatever their pastoral attitude or discipline, whatever process they may have for the recognition or even solemnization of subsequent marriages, they have to accept the decree of the secular court as a fact: to deny it, in any way which touched cognizable interests of the parties, would be to infringe a civil liberty which the courts would defend. While recognizing, from a casual acquaintance with the literature, a certain fluidity, if not disarray, in the present practice of the nullity jurisdiction in the Roman Catholic Church, it is probably true to say that nowhere are the common law and the canonical traditions further apart than in the recognition of the grounds on which a marriage is held to be validly contracted or may be validly dissolved.[5]

If the constitutional issues and divergences of practice touched upon in this chapter appear as difficulties in the ecumenical endeavour, their resolution will depend very much on the sort of approach to union or communion comtemplated. Consideration of ways and means, and of their theological and ecclesiological implications, is being pursued elsewhere, notably in the work of ARCIC supplemented at appropriate intervals by public statements, the more valued as they are the more laconic, made by the Archbishop of Canterbury and by the Pope. Discussion so far has concentrated on the ground of unity and the enquiry into impediments. Much more thought is required on the goals of unity, its form, and in what pattern of relations it should stand. No pattern looks less likely or less desirable than one to which the liturgical reformers have already mistakenly pointed, one imposing a cultural uniformity, as though it were possible, or divinely required, to obliterate differences rooted in the social, cultural and linguistic traditions which form the natural ingredients of respective local churches. This is recognized in relation to

African or Asian cultures, for example; it has been forgotten too often in respect of the assumed, but non-existent, homogeneity of the West. The consititutional implications of an ecumenical advance in England, then, will depend on the form of the chosen goal.

It happened that when, for the purpose of writing this chapter, I returned to read what I had written about Christopher St German in 1947, the editorial article which accompanied the published version of that work was a review by Dr A. R. Vidler, then Editor of *Theology*, of a Report entitled *Catholicity: a Study in the Conflict of Christian Traditions*. What he wrote then seems apposite now:

> After the word 'wholeness', the word 'synthesis' is the key-word of the Report. This was determined by the terms of reference, but we think it unfortunate. The word 'reconciliation' would be better, and probably would better express what the authors intend. 'Synthesis' suggests bringing together beliefs, notions, 'isms', into a single system of thought. Synthesizing is a human activity or ideal; God does not make syntheses. Moreover, persons and communities cannot be synthesized; but they can be reconciled. This is the work of God. The way to unity is the way of response to the Gift of God, which is the Church Universal and in which reconciliation awaits all who allow themselves to be drawn into it. And the Church Universal is not, as the Report rightly says, an *ideal*; it *is* – beneath and within all our separated churches and traditions which are at once signs and distortions of its visibility. The Report could be misinterpreted as implying that the wholeness of the Church was in the primitive period and will not be again until theologians have reached a new synthesis. Whereas what we take it to mean is that the Holy Spirit is calling us all out of separation and one-sidedness into the fellowship of the total Church which is there before us, which is the foundation on which we all stand despite our different superstructures, and in which alone we shall be in a position to appropiate the truth in its fulness since that can be received only in the fulness of communion.[6]

Not for the first time, I find past wisdom pointing a present course.

NOTES

1 This chapter was first written as a paper, at the invitation of the Canon Law Society of Great Britain and Ireland, to whom it was read in July, 1981; it is printed, slightly revised, by kind permission of the President of the Society, Monsignor Ralph Brown, to whom thanks are returned.

2 References, and fuller treatment of St German, may be found in a review which I wrote when the process of revising the canon law of the Church of England began, in 1947: *Theology* vol. L (Aug. and Sept. 1947), pp. 283ff, 324ff.

3 I would commend an excellent Catholic exposition by Olivier Loyer in a doctoral thesis, *L'Anglicanisme de Richard Hooker*. Paris, Librairie Honoré Champion, 1979. 2 vols. 991 pp.

4 Catholics may well reply that the Church of England now, in practice, does nothing at all to vindicate its orthodoxy against accredited, ordained theologians who deny certain credal foundations of the faith. The objection would be just, and debatable.

5 See *Anglican–Roman Catholic Marriage*. The Report of the Anglican–Roman Catholic Commission on the Theology of Marriage and its Application to Mixed Marriages (1976).

6 *Theology*, vol. L (1947), p. 282.

8

The Reconciliation of Memories

Mark Santer

On 1 December 1981 the Roman Catholic community in England celebrated the fourth centenary of the martyrdom of the Jesuit, Edmund Campion. Of the Elizabethan and Stuart martyrs he is probably the best known outside the Catholic community. But in the community at large the names of the earlier martyrs, John Fisher and Thomas More, are much better known, as are the Protestant martyrs, Cranmer, Latimer and Ridley. The difference is significant. Fisher and More died in the reign of Henry VIII. They were central figures in a Christian commonwealth which was not yet fragmented. They are remembered as public figures who belong to all England: Fisher, among other things, as Chancellor and great benefactor of the University of Cambridge, and More as Lord Chancellor of England. Forty-five years later, when Campion returned to England as a Jesuit missionary, he did so as a man who had deliberately rejected the Church of England to serve the cause of a persecuted minority. That is the community which has continued to remember him. To put the point differently: Anglicans do not naturally think of Fisher and More as 'Roman Catholics'. They do think of Campion, if they think about him at all, as a 'Roman Catholic'. He figures in the history of the Anglican community only as an outsider.

Most informed Anglicans are indeed scarcely aware of

the Roman Catholic martyrs who died in England between 1570 and 1680. If Campion's name is known, that is chiefly because of the biography written by Evelyn Waugh. Yet any Anglican who comes into close contact with English Catholicism will soon discover the vital importance to that community of the tradition of the martyrs. He will find a community which keeps the memory of those martyrs alive by liturgical observance and for whom it is as natural to ascribe the cause of their deaths to the Church of England as it was natural for a medieval Christian to ascribe the cause of the death of Jesus Christ to the Jews.

This I can illustrate from recent experience. A few months ago I was invited to lunch by one of the local Roman Catholic clergy – an extremely open, friendly and ecumenically-minded man. Also present was a young seminarian. I asked the seminarian why he wasn't in his seminary. He replied that they had a free day, for the feast of the Douai Martyrs. 'Who are they?', I asked. 'Some of the ones you killed', replied the parish priest.

There can be no institution to whose self-understanding these traditions are more important than the Venerable English College in Rome, founded in 1579 by Pope Gregory XIII for the training of priests for the English mission. The first name in its register of students is that of Ralph Sherwin, who was to be executed at Tyburn together with Edmund Campion, and who with Campion is now canonized as one of his Church's martyrs. I mention him because, until I spent two months as a visiting member of the College in 1979, I had never so much as heard of the generous-hearted Sherwin; yet he was the most illustrious of the 'old boys' of a foremost institution of English Roman Catholicism. He was not part of my history. Only when I had been welcomed as a member of a community of whose history his memory was a constitutive part, did he become, in a sense, part of my history.

The point of these anecdotes is to bring out the connection between our self-identification as members of particular communities and the stories we tell about the past. It is by the things we remember, and the way we remember them, and by the things we fail to remember, that we identify ourselves as belonging to this or that group. What we remember, or do not remember, moulds our reactions and our behaviour towards others at a level deeper than that of conscious reflection. This is as true of the history of families as of larger communities. It is astonishing to discover what different memories adults who are brothers or sisters will have of their common childhood. An incident at which both were present will be scarred on the memory of one, and completely forgotten by the other. Thirty or forty years later a child will still be hurt by some action to which its parents gave no further thought. The experience of neglect is particularly poignant, precisely because it cannot be deliberately intended. Marriages are likewise littered with memories, exploding like landmines under the feet of the ignorant or the careless.

It is of course notorious that warring communities have their different stories of the history which they share and which yet divides them. In the British Isles one naturally thinks of the Protestants and Catholics of Ulster. In itself it is quite natural and proper that the various groups and societies we belong to should be characterized by particular myths and stories which, like modes of dress and speech, help to form our sense of identity. Sin comes in when difference is turned into division, and when our different stories, with their distinctive emphases, distortions and omissions, are put to use for the maintenance of grievance, for self-justification and for keeping other people in the wrong. Myths sustain institutions, and institutions (such as separate schooling) sustain the myths. Sin borders on blasphemy when Christians justify their fear, loathing and persecution of each other in the name of the Christ of whom we read in the Gospel that he died to gather into one the scattered children of God. It is characteristic of such

151

divisions that we more readily remember the hurts we have received than the hurts we have inflicted; that we hold the children responsible for the sins of their fathers; and that we should be seriously put out if the 'others' were actually to repent of the sins we hold against them. All of this can be illustrated from the history of the English churches, and not only from relations between Anglicans and Roman Catholics. It is sobering, and sometimes quite a shock, for an Anglican to discover that Methodists and Roman Catholics react in the same way to the unconscious superiorities which go with 'establishment'. Anglicans think of John Bunyan as a great Christian writer; Free Churchmen think of him as a preacher persecuted by the Church of England. In the same way, part of the offence of Anglicans as perceived by Roman Catholics is that they are simply unaware of the Catholic martyrs. The same thing could undoubtedly be said about Roman Catholics in countries like Bohemia or Italy, where they have held political and social power at the expense of other Christians. It is also true that, however much we may say we want unity, most of us become alarmed when practical steps are ever proposed. This is because moving the boundaries makes us insecure.

Christians are kept apart much more by these social facts than by their ostensible theological or religious differences. To say this is not to deny or to underestimate the importance of theological arguments, nor is it to deny the centrality of the search for truth in the quest for unity in Christ. But schism occurs, not when Christians disagree, but when their disagreements take institutional form. Then, because they have a bad conscience about disunity, they tell bad stories about each other to justify their own positions. Theological arguments take their place in these stories, primarily as justifications for the status quo. Division, once institutionalized, perpetuates disputes which, within one communion, would never be seen as sufficient cause for the breaking of Christian fellowship. No 'theological' agreements between Churches will be sufficient for the restoration of communion unless they form part of a much profounder social reconciliation in which we can learn no longer to see each other as strangers but rather to trust one another as friends.

This means among other things that we must learn to tell new stories about ourselves and about one another. In other words, we need to re-educate our memories. We need to look at the past afresh.

Many Christians suppose that to attend to the past in such a way is at best an irrelevance, and at worst will serve only to keep us enmeshed in quarrels and memories we could better leave behind. It is indeed true that the present and the future are of more consequence than the past. It is also true that talk about the past can provide yet more excuses for failing to serve Christ together in the present. It is also true that the actual business of working and living together acts like nothing else in opening up a gap between inherited story and experienced reality. Nevertheless those who have actually engaged in close co-operation or community life across denominational boundaries very soon discover that they cannot escape the past; or rather they find that they cannot escape it until they have faced it. Just at the point when one party thinks that there can be no objections to a proposed course of action, he will find that it raises all sorts of spectres for the other. Differing attitudes to habits of devotion, to the exercise of authority or to the relationship between the Christian community and the world at large, reveal unquestioned assumptions, both in ourselves and in each other, of whose existence we were scarcely aware. It is when we get close to each other that we begin to discover how deeply rooted are the prejudices and fantasies through which we see one another. Sooner or later the past has to be faced. We must find out how far our prejudices conform to the facts, and what the same events look like to those who are heirs to another story. We must find out why we remember some things and others remember others. Only in this way can we get free of our fantasies.

This is above all a spiritual exercise. It is also an intellectual exercise; but it is primarily an exercise in self-examination. It is a law of the spiritual life that there is a direct proportion between the accuracy of our perception of others and the accuracy of our self-perception. To achieve a properly detached and dispassionate view of the fears and fantasies of others, we must acquire a proper detachment towards our own anxieties and needs. This is as true of a community as it is of an individual.

A classical model for growth in self-knowledge and detachment is furnished by St Ignatius Loyola in his well-known directions for examination of conscience. This takes the form of a five-finger exercise, comprising the following points: (1) thanksgiving for the favours we have received; (2) prayer for grace to know our sins and to be rid of them; (3) the examination or review, hour by hour, of the period in question; (4) prayer for forgiveness: (5) resolution to amend with the grace of God, concluding with the Lord's Prayer.

Four characteristics of this method are of particular significance to Christians who are concerned, as we are, to make of their past a source not of division but of reconciliation.

1 The process begins and ends with attention to God. It begins with thanksgiving and praise; it continues with prayer for the light of the Holy Spirit; it concludes with the Lord's Prayer, with the petition that in all things God's will may be done, and with the prayer for grace to do it. To centre everything on God, to enclose everything in attention to him, is to put everything that is not God in its proper place. The God who thus enfolds us is the God of us all.

2 It is of great importance that St Ignatius directs us to begin with thanksgiving for the favours we have received,

just as St John Chrysostom ended his life with the words, 'Glory to God for all things'. In the context of our search for unity, we do well to thank God first for the gifts we share with all Christians: the knowledge of God in Christ, the gift of the Holy Spirit, our common baptism, our mission in the world, the holy Scriptures, the example and prayers of holy men and women, and the hope of God's Kingdom. These gifts, shared in common, are infinitely more important than the things which divide us.

As well as these gifts and promises which we share with all Christians, there are the particular gifts which God has given us in England, which are also a common inheritance. There are the churches, great and small, which fill our land, still cared for with love and devotion, a visible remembrance of a time when our communion was unbroken. We have a common tradition of Christian literature and devotion. Not only do we share the treasures of a common past, *The Dream of the Rood*, Julian of Norwich, *The Cloud of Unknowing*, the miracle plays and carols of medieval England. A glance at any modern hymnbook or book of prayers will show how much we also draw on the gifts which God has given us in our separation: the poems of Donne, Southwell and Herbert, the hymns of Newman – 'Lead, kindly light' which he wrote as an Anglican and 'Praise to the Holiest in the height', which he wrote as a Roman Catholic – and the poems of T. S. Eliot. We do not only share the treasures of the past. In our own day theology and spirituality are increasingly seen as a common enterprise. We use each other's retreat houses and conference centres. We take advice and direction from each other's spiritual guides. We read each other's books – so that I was astonished to see how many copies of Bishop Michael Ramsey's addresses on *The Christian Priest Today* were to be found on students' bookshelves in the Venerable English College.

We may thank God too for the particular gifts he has given to others and which by his mercy we may enjoy: John Bunyan (who placed both Giant Prelate and Giant Pope among his ogres), Richard Baxter, Isaac Watts, Charles Wesley, P. T. Forsyth, C. H. Dodd. Where God raises up his saints and teachers, none of us can say that there is 'no church'.

This brings us to another important matter of thanksgiving. We must thank God for the diversity of his creation and for the otherness of other people. We should thank him not only for bringing us to where we are, but also for bringing others to where they are. Though we find one another baffling and at times quite incomprehensible, that is because of the limits of our own understanding and sympathy. It is human sin which turns diversity into division and which perpetuates and multiplies division by giving it institutional form, so that the sins of the fathers are visited on the children, and we go on sinning against each other. Nevertheless, despite what we do with it, our otherness remains a fundamental gift from God, and so a matter for thanksgiving. We are to enjoy what God has put into the world and into the Church, even if sin has marred it. God's creative hand does not give up when sin comes on the scene. He makes something new, for which we are also to praise him.

This matter of thanking God for our differences, even when we do not understand them, of accepting the fact that God's work in us is not yet complete, and of trusting him to bring it to perfection in his Kingdom – this is central to our ecumenical work.

3   After thanksgiving comes prayer for the illumination of the Holy Spirit. The point of this is that we should put ourselves into the hands of God before we turn to the examination of ourselves and of our past. In other words, we are not going to tell him what we have done; we are asking him to show it to us. If we tell our own story, or our forefathers' story, it will be full of self-justification and self-pity. It will be a story told against someone. St Paul's principle is crucial: we are to refrain from judgement, both

of ourselves and of others. We ask for the light of God's true and merciful judgement. So we ask for the light of the Spirit, that we may see all things in him – in both constructions of that phrase: we want to see all things by his light, as being ourselves enfolded in him; and we want to see all things, as they are enfolded in him. Thus, as we pray for light and understanding, we pray for the action of God upon us. We put ourselves into his hands.

4   It is only at this point that we turn to self-examination, or to the examination of our memories. By asking God to call the past to mind, we open ourselves to noticing facts and events of which we were scarcely if at all aware; we open ourselves to the recollection of experiences so painful that we had suppressed all memory of them; we open ourselves to the consciousness of the hurts which we or our fathers have inflicted on others; we open ourselves to the rearrangement and reinterpretation of the past.

When the individual examines his life, he tries to recollect and observe his thoughts and words and deeds as dispassionately as he can; he abstains from rewriting the story, either for praise or blame, leaving the judgement to God. This leaves space for a proper gentleness and compassion, both towards oneself and towards others. The same principle applies to our examination of our communal past. To examine the past, not in order to justify or to blame, but in order simply to understand, brings with it a gentleness and compassion towards our embattled ancestors. Protestants begin to appreciate the Catholic martyrs, and Catholics the Protestants. We begin to perceive the deep ambiguities of the situation in which all found themselves. We see that there were few really bad men, but that there were many confused and frightened men, whose vision was conditioned by their own memories and fears.

One of the most hopeful aspects of the ecumenical scene in England is that at last we are beginning to get free of apologetic history. It still hangs around, to be sure, parti-

157

cularly in regard to the sixteenth century. But historians are helping us to see the whole terrible tragedy with a greater measure of objectivity and compassion. They are helping us to see what our fathers did to each other (and to others, such as Free Churchmen), what we, following in their footsteps, have continued to do to each other, and also how we have come to do it. This can only do good. Why? Because it helps us to face our memories, our fears, our resentments and our hurts, and to face them together. There are three steps here: (i) we see more clearly and dispassionately what our fathers did; (ii) we take responsibility for their deeds, acknowledging that we are indeed their children; (iii) we face the past together with those from whom we were estranged, asking each other for forgiveness.

As we do this, we learn to see that those who suffered and died, though deeply estranged from each other in this life, died for the one faith. That the Church of England, in its revised calendar, should include both Thomas More and Thomas Cranmer as martyrs, is a sign of hope in the God who has reconciled us all to himself by the cross. So too is the fact that when Pope Paul VI canonized the Catholic martyrs of Uganda, he also remembered the Anglican martyrs who had died for the same Jesus Christ.

For Christians remembrance is an inescapable category. At the heart of our religion is obedience to the Lord's command: 'Do this in remembrance of me'. He did not tell us to forget the past, as containing memories too painful to be borne; he told us to remember it, and to find in remembrance both healing and hope. He told us to remember his death: the body given for us and the blood poured out for the forgiveness of sins. Now it is impossible to remember the night on which Jesus was betrayed without remembering who it was that betrayed him; impossible to remember his abandonment, his condemnation, his mockery and his death, without remembering who abandoned him, who judged him, who mocked him and who killed him. These things were done by men who, because they happened to be there, were acting out the fear and violence which is in us all. It is therefore impossible to remember the cross without calling our own sin to mind; or rather, it is not possible to remember the cross as a healing sacrifice, nor to appropriate it as the instrument of our own forgiveness, other than by the painful process of appropriating and repenting of our own sins. Only those who recognize their own hand in the process can recognize the body as truly given for them. Without remembrance there is no repentance; and without repentance there is no forgiveness.

This has profound consequences for our understanding of Christian and human unity. To look on the cross in faith and repentance is to see our own fear and violence made into the instrument of our peace and healing. If the Son of God has united all the pain and sorrow we inflict on each other with the pain he bore on the cross, then whenever we look with faith and repentance on the hurt we have done to one another, there too we may find the healing of the cross. If we do not own up to our deeds, we cannot be sorry for them. The tears of sorrow offered and accepted are a necessary condition for the tears of joy in reconciliation.

This life-giving remembrance of the past is inseparably linked with hope. When we celebrate the Eucharist, we remember the death of the Lord until he comes. So what we look for when, as still separated Christians, we remember our martyrs together is much more than the reconciliation of the broken fragments of the Church. Rather, what we look for is a living sign of that healing of all the sins and hurts of mankind which brought the Son of God to the cross. When by forgiving one another we have all accepted the forgiveness of God, then Christ's work in us will be done.

There are signs of this universal hope even in the bitterness of the sixteenth century. On both sides the truth was perceived that the mark of the true disciple is union with the crucified Christ. Thus that implacable Protestant,

John Foxe, introducing his account of Protestant suffering at the hand of Catholic persecution, wrote of the continuity through all the ages of 'the poor, oppressed and persecuted Church of Christ'. Edmund Campion, on the other side, was a Jesuit, a follower of Ignatius of Loyola, for whom the Christ with whom he and his companions were united was Christ poor, scorned and carrying the cross. Though men's differences ran so deep that they felt constrained to die for them, all died for the one Christ whom all tried to serve and to follow. That indeed is what makes a martyr: a martyr calls us to the imitation of Christ. The martyrs transcend our causes, our partial perceptions of the truth. They belong to us all, because they witness to the Christ who is Lord of us all.

On both sides of that rent in the body of believers, men sought to serve not a partial cause, but the universal Church of Christ. It was explicitly for the sake of the Church's catholicity that Thomas More rejected the actions of Henry VIII: 'Sith Christendom is one corps I cannot perceive how any member thereof may without the common assent of the body, depart from the common head.' But it was not only the 'Catholic' side which had a sense of the universal Church. Foxe prefaces his account of 'The Acts of God's Holy Martyrs, and Monuments of his Church' with a Calendar which includes the martyrs and confessors of the Reformation in one list with the apostles and evangelists. He had no doubt that Christ had founded a universal and continuing Church. But nothing is more eloquent than the words of Campion as he faced his death, words which speak of the fellowship of Christians as a communion of forgiven and reconciled sinners: 'Almighty God, the Searcher of Hearts sending us thy grace: Set us at accord before the day of payment, to the end we may at last be friends in heaven, where all injuries may be forgotten.'